v

Acquiring Language in a
Conversational Context

BEHAVIOURAL DEVELOPMENT:
A SERIES OF MONOGRAPHS

Series Editor
RUDOLPH SCHAFFER
University of Strathclyde
Glasgow, Scotland

Furnishing the Mind: A Comparative Study of Cognitive Development in Central
  Australian Aborigines
G.N. SEAGRIM and R.J. LENDON

Acquiring Language in a Conversational Context
C.J. HOWE

BEHAVIOURAL DEVELOPMENT:
A SERIES OF MONOGRAPHS

Series Editor: RUDOLPH SCHAFFER

Acquiring Language in a Conversational Context

CHRISTINE HOWE

Department of Psychology, University of Strathclyde
Glasgow

1981

ACADEMIC PRESS

A Subsidiary of Harcourt Brace Jovanovich, Publishers

London   New York   Toronto   Sydney   San Francisco

ACADEMIC PRESS INC. (LONDON) LTD.
24–28 Oval Road,
London, NW1 7DX

U.S. Edition Published by

ACADEMIC PRESS INC.
111 Fifth Avenue
New York, New York 10003

208516

British Library Cataloguing in Publication Data

Howe, C. J.
    Acquiring language in a conversational context. —
    (Behavioural development)
    1. Children — Language
    I. Title   II. Series
    401'.9   LB1139.L3
ISBN 0–12–356920–6
LCCCN 81–66381

Phototypesetting by Oxford Publishing Services, Oxford
and printed by
Whitstable Litho Ltd., Whitstable, Kent

Preface and Acknowledgements

Early in the 1970s, I together with many others, became excited by the idea that adult speech to children has properties that are not only unique, but are also particularly helpful to language development. Although I was happy to accept that adults produce helpful speech in many contexts, I was especially interested in whether they do this during conversations with children. The essentially two-sided nature of conversation means that anything adults achieve within it must be with the active collaboration of children. Hence, showing that children are helped by their conversational experiences would not only add to our knowledge of how language is acquired, but also help emphasize the active role that children play in the general learning process.

Accordingly around 1973, I resolved to conduct an empirical study into the nature of mother – child conversation. I hoped that once I had some insight into the properties of mother – child conversation, I could theorize about its developmental significance. I duly recruited a sample of 24 mothers and children and videotaped them in their homes on two occasions towards the end of the children's second year. I attempted a descriptive analysis of their conversations and, somewhat to my surprise, found that they produced three distinct conversational styles. Moreover, subsequent theoretical analysis suggested that some of these styles might be more helpful for language development than others. Further investigation of the children's linguistic skills supported this suggestion to some considerable extent. A few aspects of the study were reported as early as 1975 in my Cambridge University doctoral dissertation. Other sections have appeared in isolated papers. However, this book represents a first attempt to present the study as a whole and to describe its full theoretical background.

Many individuals and institutions helped me during the seven years leading up to the book. At this point, I should like to acknowledge and thank them all. The data could not have been collected without the cooperation of the mothers and children who acted as my research and pilot subjects. They all cheerfully allowed me (together with my recording equipment!) to have the free run of their homes for upwards of six hours. The data could equally not have been collected, let alone analysed, without equipment and technical assistance from the Education and Psychology Departments of Cambridge University, and from Peter Huitson. I am deeply indebted to all these people. Many people also contributed directly or indirectly to the preparation of the final manuscript. Firstly, I was encouraged to proceed by the helpful comments of my doctoral supervisor, David Bruce, and my doctoral examiners, Jerry Bruner and Martin Richards. Revisions of the various drafts were aided by suggestions from Hans Furth, many colleagues at Strathclyde University, (especially Rudolph Schaffer and David Warden), an anonymous reviewer and my husband, Willie Robertson. Again, I should like to express my gratitude to them all. Finally, there is one person I am unable to thank. My father, Walter Howe, gave considerable support to me in all my academic enterprises. Sadly, he died in October 1978. I should, however, like to dedicate this book to his memory.

Christine Howe
Glasgow 1981

Contents

1 Conversation in Mother – Child Interaction

By the time they are born, children can perform various simple actions. They can grasp, kick, stare and suck. Above all, they can vocalize. Their vocalizations are not simply the cries of hunger and pain. They are also a miscellany of sounds that seem remarkably like the elements of some natural language. At first, these sounds are used indiscriminately. However, they will soon be tied to particular situations. Well before the end of their first year, children will produce certain sounds, such as 'papapapa' in the presence of specific events, perhaps their fathers. Around their first birthday, they will produce these sounds in the absence of associated events, ceasing only when those events occur. It is hard to avoid interpreting such uses of sound as directions to produce the events. By the middle of their second year, children will use the sounds associated with past events seemingly to inform about the events. From then onwards, they will gradually expand their ideas about the kinds of things people can be directed to do and be informed about. They will realize that people can be directed to move objects into all sorts of places instead of invariably towards themselves. They will learn that people can be informed about the properties, locations and actions of objects as well as their names.

The first two years do not only produce this progress from reactive through directive to informative use of sound. They also produce changes in the sounds used to perform these functions. Although the first sounds bear little resemblance to real words, children quickly begin to adopt conventional forms. By their first birthday, they will normally have used some sounds that parents recognize as 'proper' words, albeit 'Dada' or 'Mama'. Thereafter, they will be expanding the range of words they consider appropriate for particular communicative functions. Children who initially used 'Mummy' whenever they wanted something will begin to direct their mothers by stridently naming the various objects of desire. Soon, it will not just be a question of using a wider range of words. Starting in the latter half of their second year, children will use increasingly complex combinations of words. At two years, they will direct behaviour using expressions such as 'Up ball' and 'Me jump'. Gradually, they will introduce fully fledged imperatives, such as 'You get the book', and more courteous alternatives, such as 'Could you please get the book?' and 'Are you going to get the book?'. Similarly, they will inform about events first using rudimentary expressions, such as 'There man hat' and 'She my dolly', but eventually using well formed sentences, such as 'The cow won't go in the barn' and 'The doll had a cup of tea'. By the time they reach school age, children will not only be able to give all the kinds of direction and provide all the kinds of information acknowledged by their speech community, they will also be able to use expressions that are structurally indistinguishable for those that adult members would use. Once this happens, children are customarily regarded as having learned their native language.

In some respects, five years seems an extraordinarily short time to master something as complex as a natural language. At least, it seems so if two assumptions are made. The first is that children have no special aptitude for the task of language learning. The second is that children receive no particular help from their linguistic environment. In the 1960s, the first assumption was called into question when several writers suggested that young children are innately predisposed to acquire language. They supported their suggestion by pinpointing areas where language acquisition seems remarkably impervious to environmental influences. For instance, they reported children producing combinations such as 'Allgone ni-night' and 'Drink it the milk' that they almost certainly did not hear in adult speech. They demonstrated cross-cultural similarities in the timing and sequence of language acquisition despite huge environmental differences. Although the notion that young children have innate predisposition for learning language can probably never be disproved, its force has diminished somewhat in the more recent past. This is partly because researchers have now recognized that novel combinations and cross-cultural similarities do not necessarily reflect specific predispositions for language. They may also reflect constraints imposed by general intellectual capacities. It is also because doubts have now been raised about the second assumption, namely that children do not receive any particular help from their linguistic environment. A series of studies has been published in the 1970s that show that young children rarely experience the long-winded, rapidly spoken, poorly structured speech familiar to adults. Rather, speech to young children is shorter, simpler, slower and better structured than speech to adults and older children. Although this is particularly true of mothers' speech, it is also true of speech from fathers and older siblings.

Moreover, it has also been suggested that speech to young children does not just have a helpful form. It is also put to helpful uses. Specifically, it has been thought that other people use speech to engage children in particularly facilitative conversations. Evaluating this idea seems to involve two distinct tasks. The first is discovering the nature of conversations that involve young children. The second is assessing the utility of their characteristic features. By the end of this chapter, it should be clear that even the first task is no easy undertaking. The chapter will begin by trying to clarify the nature of conversations in general. It will suggest that conversations can contain several distinct types of 'exchange', that is occasions where several people take turns to speak. The chapter will then review the psycholinguistic literature, hoping to discover which types of exchange are experienced by young children. It will focus on children's experiences during conversations with their mothers, assuming that most children converse with their mothers more frequently than with other people. The conclusion of this review will be that the psycholinguistic literature contains very little research into conversational experiences in early childhood. As a result, the chapter will suggest that more information is required about the exchanges that characterize mother – child conversation before their role in language development can usefully be considered. It will propose reserving the latter issue for Chapter 5, by which time a new study that provides the missing information will have been presented. This study will be formally summarized at the end of Chapter 1. However, it will be informally introduced throughout because the numbered examples used to illustrate theoretical points are extracts from the videotape recordings that provided actual or pilot data for the study.

A. The nature of conversational exchanges

The art of conversation has fascinated scholars for at least 200 years. In the eighteenth century, they founded clubs to promote it; in the nineteenth century, they wrote essays to praise it; and in the early twentieth century, they published manuals to improve it. They have however rarely tried to define it. Perhaps the nearest to a definition of conversation is Schegloff and Sacks' (1973) suggestion that it is an occasion in which several people take turns to speak. Although this suggestion overlooks the special case of silent conversations in the sign languages used by deaf people, it does exclude monologues, e.g., sermons or lectures, and choruses, e.g., collective prayers or political demonstrations, from the realm of conversation. Unfortunately, it does not exclude occasions in which several people take turns to speak different languages, and it would be too broad even if it were amended to taking turns in the same language. Consequently, this section will explain what else will be happening when successive speakers are holding what, in everyday life, would be termed a conversation.

(a) Address

When successive speakers are holding a conversation, they will also be addressing each other. Thus, priest and people are not conversing in the Kyrie ('*Priest*: Lord, have mercy; *People*: Lord, have mercy'), because they are addressing God rather than each other. Proposer and opposer are not conversing in a formal debate, because they are addressing the 'Chair' rather than each other. The nursery school children who produced Piaget's (1926) 'collective monologues' were not seen as conversing because they were not thought to be addressing anyone. The speakers in (1.1) and (1.2) are not conversing because the mothers are addressing the younger children rather than the older:

(1.1)   [Mother 'winds' Deborah (3:2)[1] while Melanie (20:6) plays nearby]
        Mother: Come on, you've got wind.
                Come on, windy.
        Melanie: Yes.

(1.2)   [Mother watches Lucy (23:0) brushing doll's hair; Lucy had just said 'Hair. Hair']
        Mother: Uhm, everybody's got hair, haven't they?
        [Robert (34:15) points to me]
        Robert: That got hair.

The notion that successive speakers will be addressing each other when they are holding a conversation raises the question of what constitutes addressing. Addressing is basically a matter of directing remarks at another person or persons. It may be achieved quite literally by facing the other person(s) and gazing at them during the remark. Kendon's (1967) analysis of eye-movements during conversation suggests that speakers gaze at their addressees towards the end of remarks. Gaze may be supplemented by other person-specific behaviour. For example, speakers may change vocal pitch as they address different hearers. Remick (1976) has demonstrated that mothers' speech to toddlers is pitched higher than their speech to adults. (1.3) suggests that mothers' speech to babies may be pitched higher than their speech to toddlers:

(1.3)   [Mother and Deborah (3:2) are gazing at each other; Melanie (20:6) plays with postbox and shapes]
        Mother (high-pitched voice):
                You're cheeky.

You're teasing me, aren't you?
You're a teaser.
You're a teaser.

Melanie: Push it.
Push it.
Push it.

[Mother turns to Melanie]
Mother (lower-pitched voice):
Yeh, go on then.

However, pitch would not be used as a method of address in the absence of gaze, and perhaps the only behaviour that can supplement or replace gaze as a method of address is naming. Names can be used as methods of address in conjunction with gaze or they can be used when physical obstacles make gaze impossible. Because names have a wider field of application than gaze, they take precedence over gaze when, as in (1.4), they are at variance with gaze:

(1.4)   [Ian (23:24) is engrossed in his toys; his mother smiles at her husband who is about to leave]
Mother: Say bye-bye, Ian.
Say bye-bye.
Ian: Bye, Dad.

As Sacks (1972) points out, any individual warrants several names. For instance, I can recollect being called Dr Howe, Miss Howe, Ms Howe, Christine, Chrissie and Chris! Brown and Ford (1961) and Ervin-Tripp (1969) have shown how the choice of name depends on both the social setting and factors such as relative age and status.

Speakers usually cannot demonstrate their intention to address without gazing at or naming another person(s). The only obvious exceptions are occasions, such as telephone conversations, where the participants cannot see each other. In normal circumstances, failure to gaze at, or name another person(s), will indicate a soliloquy. Thus (1.5) is not addressed to the mother by default; it is a soliloquy:

(1.5)   [Alan (25:6) builds 'Sticklebricks'; his mother sits behind him]
Alan: Two boats. Two boats.
Four boat gone.
Four boat. Four boat.
Baby one. A boats.
Baby there a boats.
Bye-bye.

Of course, speakers will sometimes gaze at, or name, other people without intending to address them. Other people can be accidentally caught within the line of regard, or they can be the referents of a remark, as in 'Alan builds Sticklebricks'. Potential participants in conversations, and psycholinguists attempting to differentiate conversations from non-conversations, must use situational cues, such as the voluntariness of eye-movements and the intonation of names to determine their function.

(b) Topic

Although mutual address is a pre-requisite for conversation, it is by no means a sufficient condition. Participants in the greeting ceremonies described by Harré and DeWaele (1976) and the closing ceremonies described by Schegloff and Sacks (1973) take turns to address each other without conversing. Rather, they engage in closely proscribed rituals that establish the social relations necessary for conversation in the immediate and distant futures. The mothers and children in (1.6) and (1.7) take turns to address each other without conversing in the ordinary sense of the word:

(1.6)   [Mother watches Barry (24:27) building blocks]
         Mother: Build it high.
         Barry: No.

(1.7)   [Mother watches Ursula (24:22) trying to post shapes]
         Mother: Pop it in.
         Ursula: Can't. Can't. Can't.

Although some psycholinguists include directive exchanges of the kind exemplified by (1.6) and (1.7) in their definition of conversation, this seems a departure from normal usage. It is hard to imagine a series of military or medical orders ('*Doctor*: Scissors; *Nurse*: Yes, doctor; *Doctor*: Scalpel; *Nurse*: Right away, doctor; *Doctor*: Morphine. . .') being regarded as conversational. Discussions about future actions are a different matter altogether. Unlike greeting ceremonies, closing ceremonies and directive exchanges, they fulfil the second requirement for conversation. They possess topics. As Keenan and Schieffelin (1976) have pointed out, the topic of a remark is the information requested or provided by the remark. The information can be as mundane as the name of an object or as abstract as the evaluation of a theory. The information can be new to one speaker or totally familiar to both. Indeed, essayists, such as J. B. Priestley and the sociologist G. Simmel, have argued that conversation is devalued by the transmission of new information! However, both would agree that successive remarks must request or provide information if they are to be regarded as conversational.

The *wh*-question is the conventional method of requesting information and there are many ways of asking *wh*-questions. They can be asked using simple interrogatives beginning with a *wh*-word, like the child's remarks in (1.8), or ending with a *wh*-word, like the mother's final remark in (1.9):

(1.8)   [Daniel (23:5) picks doll's clothes up]
      Daniel: What's that?
                  Oh, what's that?
                  What's that?
      Mother: They're the baby's clothes, aren't they?

(1.9)   [Virginia (24:9) fingers doll's teaset]
      Mother: Where's the spoon gone, Virginia?
      Virginia: Spoon under there.
      Mother: The spoon's under where?

Wh-questions can also be asked using 'elliptical' (or incomplete) interrogatives beginning with a *wh*-word, like the mother's final remark in (1.10), or ending with a *wh*-word, like the mother's remark in (1.11):

(1.10) [Mother holds two books]
      Mother: Which book do you want to read?
                  This one or this one?
                  Which book?
      [Kevin (23:27) points to one book]
      Kevin: This one.

(1.11) [Zoe (24:26) puts hat on doll]
      Zoe: Dolly's hat.
                  Dolly.
      Mother: Dolly's what?

Finally, *wh*-questions can be asked using clauses beginning with a *wh*-word and embedded in imperatives, like the mother's remark in (1.12), or in interrogatives, like the mother's remark in (1.13):

(1.12) [Sally (20:8) looks at picture]
      Mother: You tell me what you can see there.
      Sally: A my daddy.

(1.13) [Graham (23:5) looks at picture]
      Mother: Do you know what she's doing?
      Graham: Climbing up there.

The factors encouraging the selection of one alternative rather than another have not been worked out. However, it is clear from the examples and from Brown's (1968) discussion that *wh*-questions with terminal *wh*-words are unlikely except in reply.

The statement and the yes/no-question are the conventional methods of providing information. Statements can be made using declaratives with falling intonation, like the mother's remarks in (1.14), using declaratives with rising intonation, like the mother's remark in (1.15), and using 'elliptical' declaratives, like the mother's final remark in (1.16):

(1.14) [Sally (23:8) picks hippo up]
      Sally: Elephant.
      Mother: No, he's not an elephant.[2]
               He's like Horace.
               He's a hippo.

(1.15) [Barry (21:18) points to hippo]
      Barry: On the telly.
      Mother: You've seen him on the telly?

(1.16) [Nicola (23:9) is playing with jigsaw]
      Mother: What's in this one?
      Nicola: Letters.
      Mother: Letters, yes.

Yes/no-questions can be asked using interrogatives with subject–verb inversion in the main clause, like the mother's remark in (1.17), using interrogatives with subject-verb inversion in the 'tag', like the mother's remark in (1.18), and using elliptical interrogatives, like the mother's final remark in (1.19):

(1.17) [Oliver (23:19) puts shawl on doll]
      Oliver: Snug.
               Pretty snug.
      Mother: Is she going to sleep?

(1.18) [Nazma (23:11) looks at doll]
      Mother: She went to the park, didn't she?
      Nazma: I take dolly to all the park.

(1.19) [Graham (20:19) looks at jigsaw]
      Graham: Boy. Boy.
      Mother: Is there a boy?
               Or is it a girl?
               A little girl?

Excluding the rather specialized studies on women's speech inspired by Lakoff (1974), there is little work on the reasons for choosing statements or yes/no-questions or for choosing one sub-variety rather than another. Intuitively, it seems likely that they include the degree of confidence in the truth of the information or, as Sacks *et al.* (1974) point out, the degree of pressure on the addressee to respond.

Speakers cannot usually demonstrate their intention to request or provide information unless they produce remarks that are explicitly or elliptically *wh*-questions, statements or yes/no-questions. However, they can, as many writers, including Bruner (1975a) and Labov (1972), have pointed out, produce *wh*-questions, statements and yes/no-questions without necessarily intending to request or provide information. As Searle (1969) has made clear, and as the mother's remarks in (1.20), (1.21) and (1.22) illustrate, they will usually be trying to direct behaviour when they produce *wh*-questions, statements or yes/no-questions that specify ways in which the addressee's behaviour could change:

(1.20) [Yvonne (22:0) fingers crayon]
    Mother: Why don't you draw daddy?
    Yvonne: Daddy.

(1.21) [Lucy (20:7) falls off large bicycle and sobs]
    Mother: You'd be better on the small one.
    Lucy: Uhm.

(1.22) [Wayne (20:4) looks at ball]
    Wayne: Ball.
    Mother: Are you going to get the ball?

Moreover, Downes (1977), Ervin-Tripp (1976) and Gordon and Lakoff (1971) have pointed out that speakers may also be trying to direct behaviour when they produce *wh*-questions, statements and yes/no-questions that, like the mother's remarks in (1.23) and (1.24), do not specify potential behavioural changes:

(1.23) [Ian (21:0) fingers model firemen]
    Ian: There. There.
    [Mother points to box of toys]
    Mother: What else is there?
                There's another one there, isn't there?

(1.24) [Sally (20:8) sucks doll]
    Sally: Food.
    Mother: No, that's not food.
    [Mother points to doll's bottle]
    Mother: This is the food for the baby.

In such cases, however, mother's remarks are probably multifunctional. Besides being used to direct behaviour, they are almost certainly meant to have their 'literal' function of requesting or providing information,

(c) Reply

When two or more people are holding a conversation, they will be taking turns to address each other with requests and provisions of information. However, they may, as (1.25) and (1.26) show, be taking turns to address each other with requests and provisions of information without holding a conversation:

(1.25) [Mother watches Sally (20:8); Sally stares at me]
    Mother: Here's Topsy and Tim.
    Sally: Mummy, what is this?

(1.26) [Mother points to picture of apple; Nicola (20:19) rocks doll]
    Mother: What's this, Nicola?
    [Nicola turns to mother]
    Nicola: Baby asleep.

(1.25) and (1.26) are not conversations, because the second speakers did not reply to the first.

Before specifying the conditions under which second speakers will reply to first speakers, it is important to mention that replying is not constrained by considerations relating to truth. Lies, delusions and mistakes can constitute replies, and in (1.27), Kevin appears to reply, despite producing what Clark (1973) would probably call an 'overextension':

(1.27) [Mother and Kevin (20:21) are looking at picture book]
    Mother: And what's this?
    Kevin: Door.
    Mother: That's a window.
              Window, not a door.

Likewise, replying is not constrained by considerations relating to speed. The work of Jaffe and Feldstein (1970) on the duration of speech and silence suggests that replies will usually begin within two seconds of the end of their antecedents. However, this probably reflects the fact that a longer pause will be 'awkward' and may motivate the previous speaker to continue. Given the patience of the mother in (1.28), the pause can run for much longer:

(1.28) [Mother is watching Trevor (23:24) pushing cars]
    Mother: Who are you going to see?
    Trevor: Going —
    [Trevor stares at mother for 60 seconds]
    Trevor: Going, going to gramma.

Trevor clearly replies to his mother in (1.28) despite a lengthy pause; Sally and Nicola clearly do not reply to their mothers in (1.25) and (1.26), despite what will have been correctly read as a negligible pause.

Replying is in fact constrained by the function of the previous remark. If the previous remark was used to request information, it must receive the information in reply, as in (1.29), or a declaration of unwillingness or inability to supply the information in reply, as in (1.30):

(1.29) [Mother and Graham (23:5) are looking at pictures]
      Mother: And what are they playing?
      Graham: Leapfrog.

(1.30) [Nazma (23:11) takes pieces of felt from mother]
      Mother: What are they?
      Nazma: I don't quite know them.

If the previous remark was used to provide information, it must receive evaluative feedback in reply, as in (1.31), or corrective feedback in reply, as in (1.32):

(1.31) [Sally (23:8) gives model anteater to mother]
      Sally: There's a camel.
      Mother: It's not a camel.

(1.32) [Nicola (23:9) colours pictures]
      Nicola: Another poppy.
      Mother: That's holly.
                Holly. Holly.
      Nicola: Pretty flower.
      Mother: That's a tomato.
      Nicola: Apples.
      Mother: Cherries.

Responses such as the children's remarks in (1.29) and (1.30) and the mothers' remarks in (1.31) and (1.32) might be called 'minimal replies' because they fulfil the requirements for replying and no more. So long as their responses do fulfil these requirements, second speakers can also make what might be called 'extended replies' by partially changing the topic. They can request or provide new information about the same subject, as in (1.33) and (1.34):

(1.33) [Sally (20:8) looks at picture]
      Sally: Naughty doggie. Naughty doggie.
      Mother: Uhm, he's naughty.
                What's he done?

(1.34) [Daniel (20:13) looks at doll]
      Daniel: Baby. She a baby.

She. She baby.
She's a baby.
Mother: Uhm, isn't she nice!

Alternatively, they can request or provide the same information about a new subject, as in (1.35) and (1.36):

(1.35) [Kevin (20:21) looks at picture]
    Kevin: Tree there.
    Mother: Uhm, where's the tree in our garden?

(1.36) [Barry (21:18) picks bear up]
    Barry: A tiger. Tiger.
    Mother: That's not a tiger.
               This one's the tiger.

It should be noted that the extended reply can be embedded in the same remark as the minimal reply, as in (1.37), or it can be quite separate, as in (1.38):

(1.37) [Kevin (20:21) takes puppet]
    Kevin: Dougall. Dougall. Dougall.[3]
    Mother: He's a lovely Dougall, isn't he?

(1.38) [Hayley (20.11) takes puppet]
    Hayley: Dougall. Dougall.
               Dougall, is he?
    Mother: Yes, he's Dougall.
               He's lovely, isn't he?

B. The emergence of mother – child conversation

Thus, conversations consist of exchanges where one speaker addresses another speaker with a remark that requests or provides information and that other speaker addresses the first speaker with a remark that gives a minimal or an extended reply. This means that conversations can contain four qualitatively different exchanges, depending on whether the first speaker requests or provides information and whether the second speaker gives a minimal or an extended reply. In a mother – child conversation, each of these exchanges can be initiated by a remark from either the mother or the child, making eight types of exchange altogether.

(a) Onset

'Conversation' has been defined as a series of exchanges where one speaker addresses another speaker with a request or provision of information and that other speaker addresses the first speaker with a minimal or extended reply. Assuming this definition, conversational elements have been reported in the interactions between mothers and very young children. Sugarman-Bell (1978) reported a longitudinal study into the development of object- and person-oriented behaviour. Her main finding was that the coordination of object- and person-oriented behaviour occurred towards the end of the first year. However, Sugarman-Bell also mentions that vocalizations often accompanied object/person coordinations. Since person-oriented behaviour includes gaze, this strongly suggests the onset of address around the first birthday. Preliminary observations by Trevarthen (1975, 1977) indicates that address may emerge even earlier. Using data from a home-based, longitudinal study of six children, Bruner (1975a, 1975b) described how one 12-month-old girl took turns with her mother to address approximations to 'Thank you'. However, nobody has produced evidence suggesting that children will take turns to address requests and provisions of information or replies to requests and provisions of information before the middle of their second year. It would be very surprising if they had produced such evidence. Requesting and providing information about something clearly requires the capacity to objectify, which Piaget (1955) has shown to crystalize in the latter part of the second year.

There is, however, considerable research to support Snow's (1977a) suggestion that conversation begins during the latter half of the second year. Moerk (1972, 1974, 1975, 1976) has described the verbal exchanges that occurred between 20 mothers and pre-school children during 1-hour recording sessions in their homes. He found children as young as 20 months replying to remarks in which their mothers requested information. Using data extracted from home-based videotape recordings, Ninio and Bruner (1978) observed such exchanges in the interactions between one mother and a child who was about 18 months old. Although exchanges where children reply to remarks in which their mothers provide information have not been the subject of special enquiry, there is plenty of evidence to indicate their occurrence before the second birthday. As Keenan (1977) and McTear (1978) have pointed out, both adults and children regard imitation, such as the child's remark in (1.39), as an acceptable method of giving an evaluative reply:

(1.39) [Mother and Tom (21:3) are sorting through box of model animals]
       Mother: And there's a big monkey, big monkey.
       Tom: Big monkey.

A tendency to imitate is one of the best-documented characteristics of children in their second year. It has been noted at this age by Brown and Bellugi (1964), Lieven (1972) and Rodd and Braine (1971) in their home-based recordings of three children. It occurred before the second birthday in Moerk's (1972, 1974, 1975, 1976) and Nelson's (1973a) home-based recordings of larger groups of children. Finally, it was typical of the 2-year-olds in Seitz and Stewart's (1975) laboratory study of 18 children.

A similar situation arises with exchanges where mothers reply to remarks in which their children provide information. Such exchanges have not been explicitly studied, but they have been frequently reported in one form. This is where mothers make evaluative replies by 'expanding' their children's remarks into well formed sentences. Expansion is illustrated by the mother's remark in (1.40), and has been reported during the second year by Brown and Bellugi (1964), Cross (1977, 1978), Lieven (1978a), Moerk (1974, 1975), Nelson (1973a) and Seitz and Stewart (1975):

(1.40) [Eileen (23:8) points puppet towards television]
Eileen: Skippy a telly.
Mother: That's Skippy on the telly.

Far less attention has been paid to exchanges where mothers reply to remarks in which their children request information. However, they have been described by Moerk (1974, 1975, 1976) using data from the study that has already been mentioned.

(b) Pattern

Having shown that children normally begin to converse with their mothers during the latter part of their second year, the next step is to consider the frequency with which they engage in the particular types of conversational exchange. As mentioned earlier, exchanges can vary in the extent to which the first remark requests or provides information and the second remark gives a minimal or an extended reply. Mother – child exchanges can vary in the extent to which any exchange is 'mother-initiated' with the first remark coming from the mother, or 'child-initiated' with the first remark coming from the child. Hence, this subsection will summarize what existing research reveals about the percentages of mother- and child-initiated exchanges, beginning with requests and provisions of information, and ending with minimal and extended replies.

On the basis of existing research, there are grounds for expecting the percentages of mother-initiated exchanges beginning with requests, as opposed to provisions of information, to decrease from a relatively high level as children grow older. These percentages are obviously dependent on two factors: the relative percentage of requests and provisions in mothers' speech, and the relative percentages of mothers' requests and provisions receiving replies from children. With respect to the first factor, Broen (1972) observed 10 mothers of children aged 18–26 months producing inordinately high percentages of *wh*-questions in a free-play situation. *Wh*-questions are of course the conventional method of requesting information. Remick (1976) found eight mothers of children aged 16–30 months producing proportionately more requests for information in unstructured interaction with their children than in conversation with an adult. Sachs *et al.* (1976) found the same when five students interacted with a 22-month-old child and an adult. Most important for present purposes is Savic's (1975) study of a mother's speech to her twin son and daughter. The mother was recorded for 2 hours every week when her children were between 13 and 36 months. From the mother's monthly totals of *wh*-questions, yes/no-questions and statements, it seems likely that requests for information predominated in all but the earliest months of the second year, but declined thereafter relative to provisions of information. An investigation that appears to contradict these studies was reported by Snow *et al.* (1976). These authors found that requests for information never accounted for more than 9 per cent of the remarks that 18 Dutch mothers addressed to children aged 18–38 months. However, they only considered instances where the mothers genuinely did not know the requested information. As Holzmann (1972) points out, mothers frequently request information that they already know, often because they want to test their children's knowledge. Overall then, the research indicates that the percentages of mothers' requests for information decline relative to the percentages of mothers' provisions of information as children grow older. Taken with Lieven's (1978b) finding that mothers' requests are more likely to receive replies than mothers' provisions throughout early childhood, this suggests the percentages of mother-initiated exchanges beginning with requests also declines as children grow older, relative to the percentages of mother-initiated exchanges beginning with provisions.

Existing research is far less helpful on the percentages of mother-initiated exchanges ending with minimal as opposed to extended replies. It has already been pointed out that children often use imitation to give minimal, evaluative replies and researchers such as Moerk (1974, 1975), Nelson (1973a) and Seitz and Stewart (1975) have reported that imitation declines with age. However, this does not necessarily indicate percentage increases in mother-initiated exchanges ending with extended replies at the expense of mother-initiated exchanges ending with minimal replies. Afterall, the disappearance of imitation does not preclude its replacement by other minimal, evaluative forms, such as 'Yes', 'No', 'Uhm' and even expansion.

Further, imitation is only appropriate in response to remarks that provide information, and reasons for expecting a preponderance of remarks that request information have already been given. However, there are some theoretical reasons for expecting the percentage of mother-initiated exchanges ending with extended replies to increase with age. Irrespective of whether the extension is new information about the same subject or the same information about a new subject, the child must coordinate two ideas to give an extended reply. As Piaget (1926) and Piaget and Inhelder, (1956) have pointed out, children of seven years and older will experience difficulties with this kind of coordination.

Moving on to child-initiated exchanges, current research indicates an increase in the percentage of exchanges beginning with requests for information as children grow older. There is considerable longitudinal data on the relative percentages of requests and provisions of information in children's speech. Without exception, these data are derived from frequent, home-based recordings of individual children. Using the data provided by Brown (1973) and Halliday (1975), it is clear that remarks intended to provide information will be common from the middle of the second year onwards. The data provided by Halliday (1975), Labov and Labov (1978) and Savic (1975) suggest that remarks intended to request information will be rare until much later. Assuming mothers will be no more likely to reply to remarks that request information than to remarks that provide information, this indicates a proportionate increase over time in exchanges beginning with requests for information.

Current research is much more vague about changes over time in the percentage of child-initiated exchanges ending with extended replies. The reason for this lack of clarity is the emphasis on maternal expansion alluded to earlier. Taking the summary of Slobin (1968) together with the studies of Cross (1977) and Seitz and Stewart (1975), there is good reason to expect that the frequency of expansion will normally decrease from moderately high to very low as children grow older. Unfortunately, this does not necessarily indicate a proportionate increase in extended replies. It might also reflect a change to other evaluative forms, or, less plausibly, to corrective feedback. Alternatively, it might reflect the fact that well formed replies are not counted as expansions if, like the mother's contribution to (1.41), they happen to follow well formed remarks from the child. Such remarks will obviously become more frequent as children grow older:

(1.41) [Yvonne (22:0) constructs jigsaw]
     Yvonne: It's a cat.
     Mother: There's a cat.

Until these possibilities are explored, it is hard to interpret the suggestive findings of Cross (1977). Cross analysed the verbal interactions between 16 mothers and children who were recorded while playing in their homes. They were recorded on several occasions when the children were between 19 and 32 months. Cross found age-related decreases in absolute frequency of expansion and increases in absolute frequency of extended replies. These trends could reflect age-related decreases in the percentage of minimal replies and increases in the percentage of extended replies. However, in the absence of research into the frequency of minimal replies other than expansion, it is unclear whether they actually do so.

(c) The present research

Although the evidence is fragmentary and inconclusive, it does at least suggest certain changes in the pattern of mother – child conversation. It suggests that initially a relatively high percentage of mother-initiated exchanges will begin with a remark by the mother requesting information and end with a remark by the child that simply provides the requested information. A relatively high percentage of child-initiated exchanges will begin with a remark by the child providing information and end with a remark by the mother that simply evaluates the provided information. In other words, the evidence suggests that conversations such as (1.42) will be relatively frequent in the early stages:

(1.42) [Mother watches Yvonne (25:4) feeding doll]
Mother:　What's the dolly's name?
Yvonne:　Miller.
Mother:　Miller, that's it.
　　　　　What's your name?
Yvonne:　Miller.
Mother:　What's your first name?
Yvonne:　Just Miller.

The evidence also suggests that mother-initiated exchanges will increasingly begin with a remark by the mother providing information and end with a remark by the child that both evaluates and extends the provided information. Child-initiated exchanges will increasingly begin with a remark by the child requesting information and may increasingly end with a remark by the mother that both provides and extends the requested information. In other words, the evidence suggests that conversations like (1.43) will become proportionately more frequent as children mature:

(1.43) [Barry (24:27) turns block]
Barry:　　What's that?
Mother:　A bambi.

	He's in the woods.
Barry:	Uhm, what's that bambi doing?
	What's that bambi doing?
Mother:	Having his tea.
Barry:	Having his nana.

Although proportionate increases in conversations such as (1.43) at the expense of conversations such as (1.42) might be taken as a plausible hypothesis, the available evidence does not warrant its being treated as a proven fact. There would have to be more direct evidence for its validity before this could happen. With this in mind, the next three chapters of this book will report a study whose primary aim was to see whether such evidence can be produced. The study, which has been presented in summary form by Howe (1980a, 1980b) was based on the conversations held by 24 children and their mothers. These conversations occurred when the mothers and children were videotaped for 40 minutes on two occasions while they played with toys in their own homes. The children were aged between 20 and 22 months on the first occasion and between 23 and 25 months on the second.

Chapter 2 will describe these mothers and children and explain their recruitment. It will summarize the pilot work that motivated the decision to record while mothers and children played with toys and it will justify the use of videotape. It will describe the recording sessions, the subsequent transcriptions and the attempts to locate conversations in the general flow of interaction.

Chapter 3 will describe the conversations held by these mothers and children during the first recording. It will show that taking (1.42) as the prototype of early conversation was far too simple. It was true that most mother-initiated exchanges ended with minimal replies from the children, and that most child-initiated exchanges began with provisions of information from the children. However, although mother-initiated exchanges beginning with requests for information from the mothers did figure prominently in many homes, they were virtually unknown in some. Although child-initiated exchanges ending with extended replies from the mothers were virtually unknown in several homes, they figured prominently in most.

Chapter 4 will describe the pattern of mother – child conversation in the second recording. It will report very little change from the first recording with mother-initiated exchanges beginning with varying percentages of requests for information from the mothers but ending with uniformly high percentages of minimal replies from the children. Likewise, it will show that child-initiated exchanges continued to begin with uniformly high percentages of provisions of information from the children and to end with varying percentages of extended replies from the mothers.

Thus, mother – child conversations were characterized by four types of exchange that occurred with varying frequency in both recordings. These exchanges included mother-initiated exchanges beginning with requests for information from the mothers and ending with minimal replies from the children; mother-initiated exchanges beginning with provisions of information from the mothers and ending with minimal replies from the children; child-initiated exchanges beginning with provisions of information from the children and ending with minimal replies from the mothers; and child-initiated exchanges beginning with provisions of information from the children and ending with extended replies from the mothers. Faced with this characterization, Chapter 5 will return to the question that aroused the interest in mother – child conversation in the first place: the role of mother – child conversation in child language development. It will suggest that mother-initiated exchanges beginning with requests for information should motivate children to develop certain aspects of using language to provide information. Mother-initiated exchanges beginning with provisions of information should have little impact. Child-initiated exchanges beginning with provisions of information should help the development of skill at using language to provide information irrespective of whether they end in minimal or extended replies. However, the assistance to be gained from minimal replies should be less than the assistance to be gained from extended replies.

If these proposals are correct, the children under study should vary in the assistance they received from mother – child conversation, since they varied in their exposure to the putatively helpful exchanges. Chapter 6 will present evidence compatible with this. It will show that the children who engaged in the theoretically most helpful conversations developed most rapidly in the areas of interest. Although it will be unable to consider the issue thoroughly, Chapter 6 will show that few potential influences outside the conversational context could have produced the results.

Chapter 7 will discuss some questions arising out of the study. It will start by considering the origin of variations in mother – child conversation. Although firm conclusions are impossible, Chapter 7 will discuss the theoretical and practical implications of potential origins suggesting how they might be further researched. It will then consider whether mother – child conversation could influence children's skill at performing communicative functions other than providing information. It will propose a new conceptualization of children's linguistic knowledge, which makes the issue less clear-cut than would normally be supposed.

Notes

[1]All names are pseudonyms and the children's ages are given in months and days (i.e. (3:2) = 3 months and 2 days).

[2]A fullstop (.) indicates falling intonation and a question mark (?) indicates rising intonation.

[3]Dougall is a long-haired puppet dog who featured in a popular children's television series.

2 Recordings of Mother – Child Conversation

Broadly speaking, the aim was to conduct a study that would show whether mother – child conversation changed over time in the manner suggested by previous research. There would be no hope of realizing the aim unless the study involved mothers and children who were representative of the population as a whole and unless the study elicited conversations from these mothers and children that were representative of their conversations as a whole. Hence, this chapter will begin by describing the steps taken before the recording sessions to obtain an appropriate group of mothers and children and to discover which situation would produce an adequate sample of their conversations. In addition, there would be no hope of realizing the aim of the study unless the recordings of mother – child interaction were carefully transcribed and analysed for the presence of conversation. Having described the recording procedure, the chapter will end by explaining how the recordings were transcribed and how the criteria mentioned in Chapter 1 were used to locate conversational exchanges in the flow of interaction.

A. The preparations for the study

Given the nature of previous research, there seemed strong theoretical reasons for recruiting children who were entering the latter half of their second year and therefore just beginning to converse with their mothers. There were of course fewer theoretical reasons for recruiting one number of children rather than another, and the issue of sample size was resolved by practical consideration of available time. The sampling, piloting, recording and transcribing had to be completed within a nine-month period. As a rough guide, it was assumed that sampling and piloting would take about 2 days per mother and child, and that recording and transcription would take 3 days per mother and child. It was also assumed that each mother and child would have to be recorded twice to investigate changes over time. Granted these assumptions, it was estimated that 24 mothers and children could be recorded on two occasions, 3 months apart, within the available nine months. A smaller sample could obviously be recorded with a larger time interval. However, a 3-month interval seemed adequate, given the speed of development in the latter half of the second year, and the maximum sample seemed desirable in the interests of representativeness. Hence, an attempt was made to recruit a sample of 24 mother – child pairs.

(a) Subjects

The most straightforward method of obtaining a reasonable sample of mothers and children would have been random or quota sampling from a local authority list. Unfortunately, the local authority in question refused to cooperate and more indirect methods had to be used. As a start, an article was written for the local newspaper explaining the aims of the study in deliberately vague terms and asking mothers to volunteer children in the age range 15–18 months. Notices making similar requests were posted in likely public places, including doctors' waiting rooms, baby clinics, university common rooms and centres for further education. A social worker persuaded one of her clients to take part. Finally, a month after recruitment had started, health visitors from two of the baby clinics made contact with offers of help. One suggested sitting in on an afternoon session and asking attending mothers to participate. This was done. The other offered names and addresses of every mother with a child of the right age in her area. The first eight in the alphabetical list were contacted and six said they were interested in taking part. By this time, some of the first volunteers had marshalled their friends into participating, and at the end of the period available for sampling, 33 mothers had volunteered their children. Two mothers were considered unsuitable because they had delegated childcare to a grandmother and an employed nanny. The remaining mothers had volunteered children in the age range 13–21 months. It seemed sensible to choose the mothers with the 24 children nearest in age to the mean of 17 months and use the others for pilot work.

Most of the final group lived in a small university-cum-market town although some lived in nearby villages. Despite the fact that sampling was anything but random, the group was a satisfactorily well mixed bunch by sex of child, birth order of child and social class of family. Twelve children were boys and 12 were girls. Seven were only children, seven were the youngest of two, four were the oldest of two, four were the youngest of three and two were twins without other siblings. Of course, none of the children came from large families, but then large families are relatively uncommon in contemporary Britain. At the time of the 1971 Census, which was carried out two years before the data were collected, only 8.5 per cent of all families had four or more children. The fathers of 13 children had professional or managerial occupations, whereas the fathers of the remaining 11 children had skilled or semi-skilled manual occupations. Given the high correlations between paternal occupation and other indices of social status reported by Kohl and Davis (1955) and Lawson and Boek (1960), it seemed reasonable to call the first group 'middle class' and the second group 'working class'. Unrepresented were families where the father was unemployed or an un-skilled manual worker. The omission of families with fathers in the latter category may seem unfortunate given the extensive discussion of their linguistic skills in Bernstein (1971). However, it must be remembered that they, too, are a small group, amounting to 6.6 per cent of the working population at the time of the 1971 Census. Table 2.1 shows the sex, birth order, social class and recruitment method of the children (all identified by pseudonyms).

Table 2.1. *Sex, birth order, social class and recruitment method of children in sample*

Name	Sex	Birth Order	Social Class	Method
Alan	Male	2nd of 2	Working	Clinic
Barry	Male	3rd of 3	Working	Clinic
Caroline	Female	3rd of 3	Middle	Clinic
Daniel	Male	Only	Middle	Notice
Eileen	Female	Only	Working	Clinic
Faye	Female	1st of 2	Middle	Other Mother
Graham	Male	1st of 2	Middle	Notice
Hayley	Female	Only	Working	Other Mother
Ian	Male	2nd of 2	Working	Article
Jason	Male	1st of 2	Middle	Notice
Kevin	Male	2nd of 2	Middle	Article
Lucy	Female	2nd of 2	Middle	Other Mother
Melanie	Female	1st of 2	Working	Clinic
Nicola	Female	3rd of 3	Working	Clinic
Oliver	Male	Only	Middle	Other Mother
Philip	Male	2nd of 2	Working	Article
Richard	Male	2nd of 2	Middle	Article
Sally	Female	Only	Middle	Article
Tom	Male	Twin	Middle	Clinic
Ursula	Female	Twin	Middle	Clinic
Virginia	Female	3rd of 3	Working	Notice
Wayne	Male	Only	Working	Article
Yvonne	Female	Only	Working	Social Worker
Zoe	Female	2nd of 2	Middle	Notice

(b) Activity

Having chosen the mothers and children, the next problem was deciding when to record them. Since they could not be recorded for the whole day everyday, they had to be recorded performing some activities rather than others, and great care had to be taken over the choice of activities. Studies reviewed by Cazden (1970) and Ervin-Tripp (1969) have shown how the activity affects many aspects of the verbal interaction, including fluency, mean length and grammatical complexity of utterances, and choice of vocabulary items. In a study of mothers' speech to 42 children aged between 11 and 24 months, Messer (1978) found that the topic of conversation was strongly influenced by ongoing activity. For instance, over three quarters of all references were to toys held by mother or child. Consequently, it seemed imperative to make the present recordings while the children were performing activities that occupied a significant part of their daily lives. To find out which activities did this, four hours were spent in each home noting how much time was spent on the 15 activities listed in Table 2.2. Pilot work had shown that these activities are the main occupations of young children.

Table 2.2. *Popularity of possible activities for recording*

	Percentage of total time		Rank	
	Mean	Standard deviation	Mean	Standard deviation
Playing with toys	29.07%	11.00	1.50	0.89
Playing with household objects	15.71%	11.01	3.15	1.57
Looking at books	9.01%	9.04	6.03	3.22
Drawing	1.63%	4.24	11.10	3.17
Playing with animals	0.87%	1.37	11.38	3.12
Listening to television, radio and records	9.37%	12.40	7.95	5.36
Eating	12.11%	7.61	3.98	2.60
Drinking	4.15%	3.56	6.73	2.29
Washing	1.44%	2.09	9.50	2.43
Dressing	4.90%	4.25	6.40	2.39
Sitting on potty	2.06%	5.59	11.63	3.43
Washing up	1.07%	1.65	10.40	3.27
Washing laundry or ironing	1.42%	2.31	10.60	2.85
Cleaning	1.37%	3.16	11.20	3.19
Cooking	2.62%	2.90	8.43	2.48

In the first four homes, an unsuccessful attempt was made to note activities using an 'event recorder', a device that requires pressing keys to signal the onset of an activity. In the remaining 20 homes, a simpler and altogether more successful method was used. All it involved was reading the time at which an activity began and ended from a stopwatch and noting it on a paper grid with columns marked for the 15 activities and rows marked for each 15-second period in 4 hours. Because this method was so straightforward, the observer could easily note activities for four hours without losing concentration. However, it was sometimes impossible to observe for the full 4 hours because the children became tired. Partly for this reason and partly because there was sometimes more than four hours' worth of data, because of overlapping activities, the percentage of total 15-second periods devoted to each activity was used for the analysis rather than the absolute number of 15-second periods.

The purpose of the analysis was to find an activity for the recordings proper that occupied the children for sizeable periods of their daily lives. If the children differed markedly in the percentage of time they devoted to the activities, several activities would have to be incorporated in the recordings. Every child would have to be recorded performing his or her favourite activity and the favourite activities of the other children. If the children did not differ markedly, they could be recorded performing the same activity. To measure the agreement across children, the activities were ranked for the percentage of total time devoted to them by each child, and Kendall's coefficient of concordance (Siegel, 1956) was computed. The agreement turned out to be high ($W = 0.541$; $\chi^2 = 151.701$; df $= 14$; $p<0.001$)[1], meaning that a single activity could be used for all the children. As Table 2.2 shows, the highest ranking activity when the ranks were averaged across children turned out to be 'playing with toys'. Its average ranking was 1.50; it was the most popular activity for 14 children, the second most popular for three children, the third most popular for two children and the fourth most popular for one child. It occupied 29.1 per cent of the total time on average, and overall there seemed every reason to accept it as the activity for the recordings.

The decision to record while the children played with toys raised the question of whether the toys should be specially provided. There were several reasons for bringing a special set. They would mean that the operator and her equipment were not the only novel features in the room. They might help to ensure that the whole recording session was devoted to playing with toys without any forcible restraint. On the other hand, the toys might be more familiar to some children than to others and hence introduce new biases. In the end, a compromise was reached and the children's own toys were used for the first half of the recording session and a special set was used for the other half. Great care was taken to make this special set as varied, yet familiar as possible. The special set consisted of:

1. Jigsaw puzzle.
2. Plastic postbox with holes in the top for geometric shapes.
3. Plastic doll with clothes, teaset, cot and brush.
4. Lorry.
5. Jeep and horsebox.
6. Model zoo animals with fences, cages and keeper.
7. Interchangeable heads, arms and legs which could be assembled into postmen, firemen and policemen.
8. Cardboard building blocks with pictures on every face.
9. Fluffy puppet.
10. Picture story.

The toys were packed in a cardboard box in a specific order so that all the children would find them in the same order.

(c) Technique

Although the focus was on verbal interaction, non-verbal information would be needed, for several reasons. Firstly, it would probably be needed to determine address. Although address can be signalled by naming, it seemed likely that many remarks would not be accompanied by names. Hence, information about eye-movements would be needed to decide whether these remarks were being addressed by gaze. Secondly, non-verbal information would be needed to decide whether incomplete remarks were elliptical *wh*-questions, yes/no-questions or statements, and whether *wh*-questions, yes/no-questions and statements were intended to request or provide information rather than direct behaviour. As mentioned in Chapter 1, a crucial factor in determining the function of these speech forms is the relation between actions specified by verbs and actions being performed by addressees. Thirdly and less centrally, non-verbal information would be useful for identifying speakers in the case of the twins. Finally, it would show whether mother – child conversation was being artifically constrained by micro-factors such as choice of toy.[2] This might seem a distinct possibility in the light of research by Messer (1978), summarized earlier in this chapter.

The required non-verbal information would amount to every action (including gaze) and focal object of both mother and child. The exact time at which new actions occurred and/or new objects were adopted would have to be recorded for coordination with the records of verbal interaction. There seemed little doubt that such precise information would have to be recorded when it occurred and not added from memory as Wells (1974) has done in a study with less exact requirements. However, there was some uncertainty over whether the required information could be reliably recorded by an observer using a paper-and-pencil technique or whether a videotape recorder would have to be used. Many writers, including Gewirtz and Gewirtz (1965, 1969), Richards and Bernal (1972) and Walters *et al.* (1964), have used paper-and-pencil techniques to record the time period during which particular actions occurred. Some writers, including Heinicke (1956) and Leach (1972), have used paper-and-pencil techniques to record the time period during which particular objects were focused upon. No writers have reported using paper-and-pencil techniques to record both the onset of actions and the adoption of objects, let alone the exact time at which they occurred. After sustained failure to use paper-and-pencil techniques to perform this feat for one actor not to mention two, the absence did not seem in the least surprising! In the event, there seemed no alternative but to use a videotape recorder despite considerable misgivings about the lack of mobility and the level of distraction it seemed likely to cause.

B. The procedure of the study

Although the preparatory work took several months, it seemed to be time well spent. It provided an activity that was familiar to all the children and it meant that the investigator had become acquainted with the mothers and children before the proper recording sessions. It may be one reason why this section will show that many of the anxieties about videotape seemed unfounded. This was despite the fact that only two mothers (the wives of a television delivery man and an electrician) had seen or heard of videotape.

(a) Recording

The recordings were made on two occasions, once when the children's ages to the nearest month were 20–22 months and again when their ages to the nearest month were 23–25 months. Nineteen mother – child pairs were recorded between 10.00 am and 11.00 am and five were recorded between 2.30 pm and 3.30 pm. The time of day guaranteed that few people besides the mothers, the children and younger (non-verbal) siblings were present. However, older siblings contributed to five recordings and father, lodgers, neighbours and grandmothers were silently present during six recordings. Before the recordings began, the mothers were told that they would be in two 20-minute sessions, the first using the children's own toys and the second using the specially provided toys. The rationale for using two sets was explained, but the mothers were not told, and indeed had not been told on previous occasions, that their own speech was of interest. Instead, they were asked to act as naturally as possible during the recording sessions.

Once the recording equipment had been established in the living room and the mother had put out some of the child's own toys, the operator pretended to record. The actual recordings did not begin until some (generally short) time later when the child and the mother seemed settled. The first tape ended after about 20 minutes and, when it had been replaced with a fresh tape, the box of toys was produced. If the mothers requested more information about what they should do with the special toys, they were asked to act as they might normally do on other occasions, such as birthdays and Christmas, when a new set of toys arrived. This seemed a way of acknowledging that the situation was special, but encouraging the mothers to assimilate it to something with which they were familiar. The special-toy session, like the first session, lasted until the tape ran out (approximately 20 minutes). There was no possibility of randomizing the order of sessions, because the children would never have relinquished the special toys after 20 minutes. There was absolutely no constraint on anybody to stay in the room. The children tended not to run out when they were playing with the special toys. Some of the mothers did leave for short periods of time to answer telephones, pay tradesmen and complete small domestic chores. If the participants split up, the convention was to follow the child even if this meant moving out of the room.

Despite all these precautions, it is possible that the recordings were not entirely naturalistic. In the first place, they could have encouraged the mothers and children to increase or decrease the frequency of their habitual behaviour. However, this would not create problems, since the analysis was going to be based on percentage rather than absolute frequency. Secondly, the recordings could have encouraged the mothers and children to adopt new behaviour patterns, and this would, of course, cause difficulties. Although there is no ultimately conclusive check for this kind of distortion, it should be pointed out that the recordings compared well with casual observations made during the 4-hour sessions that were surely too long for anyone to put on an act. The occasional shows of swearing and physical punishment suggested spontaneity. Two mothers who were next-door-neighbours behaved as they had described each other and most of the mothers expressed pleasant surprise at how quickly they and their children forgot about the recording equipment. When the equipment and its operator were not forgotten, they were discussed much like any other objects. The conversation in (2.1) was typical:

(2.1)   [Virginia (21:17) fingers videotape recorder]
         Virginia: Hot. Hot. Hot.
                       Hot. Hot.

Mother: Is it hot?
Virginia: Hot. Hot. Hot.
Mother: Is it?
Virginia: Hot.
Mother: Is it?
[Andrew (36:4) touches videotape recorder]
Andrew: It isn't.
Virginia: Hot. Hot. Hot.

The single attempt to incorporate the operator in the interaction and its consequences appear in (2.2):

(2.2)   [Mother takes tea-cup from Richard (25:9)]
    Mother: Perhaps Christine would like some.
                  Christine have a cup of tea?
    Richard: Eh doesn't want it.
    Mother: Doesn't she want any?
                  Did you ask her?
    Richard: No, eh doesn't want it.
    Mother: She doesn't, no.
                  You can say 'Christine, would you like a cup of tea?'.
    Richard: Eh buzzing, buzzing.
    Mother: She's busy, is she?
    Richard: Yes.
    Mother: Too busy buzzing.

(b) Transcription

Once the recording sessions had finished, the tapes were brought to a soundproof laboratory for immediate transcription. They were rewound and played back in the order of recording on a videotape recorder connected to a television screen and an audiotape recorder. The transcriber sat 6 feet from the screen holding an electrically powered pad that moved paper across a frame at the rate of 6 inches per minute. The rolls of paper used with this device had lines at ¼-inch intervals. Thus, it was possible to know within 2½ seconds when any mark on the paper was made, and 2½ seconds became the basic time interval for the analysis.

The moving-paper device, the audiotape recorder set to record and the videotape recorder set to playback were started in that order. Watching only the child, the transcriber noted changes of action and object using a short-hand code. This code was evolved through pilot work, and essentially used hieroglyphics to represent actions, including gaze, and the first two letters of names to represent the objects of actions. Every time the child vocalized, a dash was drawn on the left of the paper to be filled in later. Every vocalization, was of course, being re-recorded on audiotape. The second tape was replayed and the child's behaviour transcribed in the same way. Then the audiotape recorder was switched off and the whole procedure repeated for the mother. The transcription of the twins and all other participants required a third run.

The next stage was transcribing the vocalizations and inserting them in the behavioural record. Unlike the videotape recorder, the audiotape recorder could be safely stopped and started, so the transcription proceeded not at the rate of events, but laboriously until an accurate record had been made or an utterance was considered totally unintelligible. English words were transcribed as English words and other sounds were transcribed with some attempt to represent them using English syllables. Speakers varied in their intelligibility, and the tapes varied in the amount of background noise. The mean percentage of intelligible utterances was 94.96 per cent with a standard deviation of 5.30 for the children, and 98.11 per cent with a standard deviation of 2.84 for the mothers. There was never any problem in deciding whether mothers or children were speaking. However, difficulties did arise with the twins and to a lesser extent, with older siblings. Here, the practice was to transcribe the problematic remark and re-run the videotape to find out who had made it. Once the vocalizations had been transcribed, they were inserted on the behavioural records as indicated by the dashes.

One year after the final recording, the transcription code was relearned and extracts from the tapes transcribed once more. The focus of the research was on verbal interaction, so a reliability coefficient was calculated by comparing the percentage agreement between the two transcriptions over the content and sequence of speech and other vocalizations. The comparison was extremely strict. If there was disagreement over a single word in a sentence or even over the inclusion of an 'Oh' or an 'Uhm', an error was counted. There would have to be more serious disagreement than this before the validity of the claims to follow would be affected. Nevertheless, the percentage agreement between the two transcriptions was 91.52 per cent. Another reliability coefficient was produced by calculating the percentage agreement over the non-vocal behaviour and speech in every 2½ second period during which speech occurred. There was no point in considering any other 2½ second periods, because the interest was in the immediate non-vocal context of speech. Again, the comparison was perhaps excessively stringent. If the synchronization of non-vocal behaviour and speech was only 2½ seconds out of step, an error was counted. Once more however, the agreement of 83.70 per cent was acceptably high.

(c) Conversation

When the transcription was complete, it became clear that the videotapes had lasted between 20 and 23 minutes, making recordings that varied in length from 40 to 46 minutes. Since recordings of equal length would simplify the quantitative analysis quite considerably, it seemed sensible to ignore speech that occurred after the first 20 minutes of every tape. As Table 2.3 shows, the remaining speech from the mothers consisted of between 37 and 371 remarks in the first recording, and between 13 and 423 remarks in the second. The remaining speech from the children consisted of between 68 and 414 remarks in the first recording and between 160 and 496 remarks in the second. Using these remarks, the children's speech was subjected to several standard though (as subsequent chapters will imply) perhaps rather superficial, measures of language development. Mean length of utterance in morphemes (MLU) was computed using the rules devised by Brown (1973). Type-token ratio for words (TTR) was computed by dividing the total number of words into the total number of different words. The result of these computations are given in Table 2.4.

Table 2.3. *Total number of remarks in forty minutes*

	Mother		Child	
	1st Recording	2nd Recording	1st Recording	2nd Recording
Alan	160	13	150	160
Barry	204	155	224	242
Caroline	51	163	212	258
Daniel	135	314	230	165
Eileen	50	194	140	246
Faye	140	88	210	312
Graham	120	230	296	351
Hayley	101	210	166	258
Ian	175	186	304	219
Jason	94	226	107	367
Kevin	324	306	285	327
Lucy	40	168	84	275
Melanie	37	80	351	272
Nicola	257	423	68	403
Oliver	325	303	205	496
Philip	170	328	174	250
Richard	80	249	414	224
Sally	281	314	286	395
Tom	371	363	124	190
Ursula	371	363	153	174
Virginia	308	256	235	256
Wayne	204	328	205	380
Yvonne	200	226	222	316
Zoe	218	198	127	268

Table 2.4. *Some standard measures of the children's language development.*

| | 1st Recording | | 2nd Recording | |
	MLU[a]	TTR[b]	MLU[a]	TTR[b]
Alan	1.16	0.24	2.05	0.21
Barry	1.30	0.27	2.56	0.20
Caroline	1.42	0.30	1.71	0.30
Daniel	1.44	0.27	2.03	0.24
Eileen	1.47	0.18	1.57	0.38
Faye	1.27	0.17	1.65	0.23
Graham	1.09	0.26	1.32	0.51
Hayley	1.36	0.29	1.98	0.36
Ian	1.53	0.38	2.04	0.41
Jason	1.00	0.17	1.17	0.40
Kevin	1.16	0.45	1.87	0.50
Lucy	1.09	0.17	1.15	0.23
Melanie	1.19	0.43	1.55	0.41
Nicola	1.21	0.21	1.67	0.55
Oliver	1.53	0.23	2.04	0.23
Philip	1.22	0.17	1.54	0.26
Richard	1.30	0.16	2.13	0.19
Sally	1.33	0.39	1.98	0.44
Tom	1.27	0.30	3.00	0.21
Ursula	1.09	0.36	2.80	0.23
Virginia	1.40	0.38	1.50	0.46
Wayne	1.33	0.18	1.39	0.26
Yvonne	1.72	0.26	3.03	0.33
Zoe	1.13	0.36	1.69	0.37

[a]Mean length of utterence in morphemes.
[b]Type-token ratio for words.

These measures should show how the children in the present sample compare with children reported in other studies. Although this should be useful, it is not of central importance for the present analysis. It is much more important to see how the children's remarks were used in conversation. As pointed out in Chapter 1, conversations contain series of exchanges (which might be called 'conversational exchanges') where the first speaker addresses the second speaker with a remark that requests or provides information and the second speaker addresses the first speaker with a remark that gives a minimal or an extended reply. The analysis proceeded by trying to locate these exchanges in the overall flow of mother – child interaction. As a first step, an attempt was made to differentiate remarks that the mothers and children did and did not address to each other. It was assumed that children in the present age range would know that gaze and/or names are the conventional methods of address. The work of Sugarman-Bell (1978) and Bruner (1975a, 1975b, 1977), outlined in Chapter 1, has suggested that gaze is used to signal address around the first birthday. The work of Dore (1974, 1975) and Halliday (1975) indicates that names are used for this purpose at about the same time. Nevertheless, it was recognized that neither the children nor the mothers would be addressing every time they gazed at or named each other. Hence, situational cues would be needed to determine the function of person-directed gazes and names. Because the non-verbal record provided these cues, it was usually easy to select instances where address was the only plausible function of a gaze or a name. The main difficulty was with isolated names like 'Mummy'. In isolation, names lack the tell-tale intonation contour that allowed writers such as Bloom (1970) and Bowerman (1973) to determine their function in remarks as simple as 'Mummy sock'. Luckily, isolated names were rare in the speech of both mothers and children. When they occurred, they were usually regarded somewhat arbitrarily as terms of address.

Once remarks that the mothers and children addressed to each other had been located in this not-altogether satisfactory manner, the next problem was to divide them still further into remarks that did and did not request or provide information. As explained in Chapter 1, information is conventionally requested using *wh*-questions and conventionally provided using statements or yes/no-questions. From existing research, it seemed highly likely that the present children would know of these conventions. Ervin-Tripp (1970) found that 2-year-olds respond appropriately when adults use *wh*-questions to request information. Klima and Bellugi (1966) and Piaget (1962) report children using *wh*-questions to request information around their second birthday. Bever (1970) has shown that 2-year-olds can act out situations described in statements, and many writers, including Bloom (1970, 1973), Bowerman (1973), Greenfield and Smith (1976) and Rodgon (1976), have reported children between 1½ and 2 years making rudimentary statements that can only be interpreted as providing information. However, it would be naive to assume that every *wh*-question, statement or yes/no-question from the children, let alone from the mothers, was concerned with information. It has already been pointed out that these speech forms can take a directive function in certain circumstances. Therefore, the non-verbal contexts of the remarks under consideration were scrutinized to see whether these circumstances prevailed. There were no instances where the children seemed to use *wh*-questions, statements and yes/no-questions to direct behaviour. As might be expected from the work of Broen (1972), Schaffer and Crook (1979) and Shatz (1978), however, the mothers seemed to use *wh*-questions, statements and yes/no-questions for this purpose on many occasions. For instance, the non-verbal context makes every *wh*-question, statement and yes/no-question produced by the mother in (2.3) seem directive:

(2.3) [Richard (25:9) has just been hitting mother with hammer]
    Mother: Would you like to draw me a picture?
    Richard: Oh yes.
    Mother: Or would you like to play the 'cello?
               Or perhaps you'd like to play the piano.
    Richard: Oh yes.
    Mother: Play us a tune, Richard.
               You'd like to play a tune, wouldn't you?
               Not with a hammer on the piano.
               Play with your fingers like daddy does.
               Why not play a tune?
    Richard: Don't sing.

If it would have been naive to assume that all *wh*-questions, statements and yes/no-questions were concerned with information, it would have been absurd to assume that all attempts to request and provide information would be made with well formed *wh*-questions, statements and yes/no-questions. Again, as pointed out in Chapter 1, incomplete remarks can be used to request or provide information. Like their counterparts in the studies of Broen (1972), Holzman (1974) and Snow (1972), the mothers rarely produced incomplete remarks. However, the children's speech abounded with such remarks and the non-verbal context was frequently invoked to decide their function. Again, inherently ambiguous remarks were counted as requesting or providing information.

Thus erring once more on the side of optimism, the analysis had now produced a series of remarks in which the mothers and children appeared to address each other with requests and provisions of information. The final problem was deciding whether these remarks received replies when they were followed by a change of speaker. To reiterate points made in Chapter 1, replying to remarks that request information entails providing or declining to provide the information. Replying to remarks that provide information entails evaluating or correcting the information. If these 'minimal' requirements are fulfilled, more 'extended' replies can be made by requesting or providing new information about the same subject or the same information about a new subject. On the basis of the research mentioned in the previous paragraph, it seemed reasonable to assume that the children under study, as well as their mothers, would rarely fulfil either the minimal or the extended requirements for replying without intending to do so. Hence, the mothers and children were taken as replying when they fulfilled these requirements, unless there was a very good reason for assuming otherwise, as in (2.4):

  (2.4) [Mother and Sally (23:8) gaze in my direction; a wooden antelope stands on
          shelf behind me]
        Mother: That's Christine.
        Sally: Animal.

Although the child's remark was interpreted as a label for the antelope and therefore a non-reply, it could have been intended as a rather insulting alternative to 'Christine'! Fortunately, the circumstances creating such ambiguities were rare.

At this point in the analysis, a series of mother – child exchanges had been located that appeared to be conversational. In other words, these exchanges began with the first speaker seeming to address the second speaker with a remark that requested or provided information. They ended with the second speaker seeming to address the first speaker with a minimal or extended reply. Sometimes, the mothers and children produced solitary conversational exchanges in the middle of non-conversational speech. For example, only the final exchange of (2.5) was regarded as conversational; all the others violate at least one of the requirements for conversation:

  (2.5)   [Virginia (24:9) fights with Andrew (40:6) over doll]
       Virginia: No.
       Andrew: Why?
       Virginia: No.
       Andrew: Do it.
       Virginia: No. No.
       Mother: I think you'd better leave our baby alone; she's a possessive
               mother
       Virginia: A baby.
       Mother: It's your baby, is it?

At other times, the mothers and children produced strings of conversational exchanges, such that remarks constituting replies in one exchange counted as initiatory requests or provisions in the next. These strings were far from the virtuosi coordinations that Coulthard (1977) has shown to occur in adult conversations. As will become apparent in Chapter 3, they often arose because imitative acknowledgments from the children received imitative or extended replies from the mothers, as in (2.6):

  (2.6)   [Oliver (23:19) puts shawl on doll]
       Mother: Is she going to bed?
       Oliver: Go to bed.
               Snug. Snug.

Mother:	Snug, yes.
Oliver:	Snug.
Mother:	Snug as a bug.
Oliver:	A bug.
Mother:	Uhm, in there.
Oliver:	There. There.

Reviewing the analysis, it is highly likely that some non-conversational exchanges were regarded as conversational. It is also conceivable, although less likely in view of the policy of including unclear cases, that some conversational exchanges were regarded as non-conversational. Since these incorrect decisions reflect the inherent ambiguity of speech, they will not be rectified by pooling the opinions of several judges. They must be accepted as inevitable. However, they were almost certainly sufficiently rare and random across mother – child pairs to avoid serious distortion in the next stage of the analysis. The next stage began by dividing conversational exchanges into those initiated by remarks from the mothers and those initiated by remarks from the children. It then proceeded by calculating the percentages of mother- and child-initiated exchanges that began with requests rather than provisions of information and ended with extended rather than minimal replies. The results of these calculations on data from the first recordings are given in Chapter 3.

Notes

[1] The conventional abbreviations for statistics will be used throughout. Thus, $W =$ Kendall's coefficient of concordance; $\chi^2 =$ Chi-squared; df = Degrees of freedom; p = Probability.

[2] To save space, this analysis will not be described in this book, since it is reported in Howe (1975). Suffice it to say that none of the results to be presented in subsequent chapters could be artefacts of micro-factor constraints.

3 Conversational Exchanges in the First Recording

The procedures described in Chapter 2 produced a series of mother – child exchanges that were believed to be conversational. In other words, these exchanges began with the first speaker addressing the second speaker with a remark that appeared to request or provide information. They ended with the second speaker addressing the first speaker with a remark that appeared to give a minimal or an extended reply. Faced with these exchanges, the next question must be what percentages began with requests rather than provisions of information, and ended with minimal rather than extended replies. This and the next chapter will be concerned with answering that question, by presenting the percentages for conversational exchanges initiated by remarks from firstly the mothers and secondly the children. This chapter will give the percentages from the first recordings of the 24 mother – child pairs, whereas the next chapter will give the percentages from the second recordings.

At the time of the first recordings, the children were only 20–22 months old, and would have just started to converse with their mothers. Research summarized in Chapter 1 gave one or two hints about these early conversations, which might usefully be reiterated at this stage. The research suggested that conversational exchanges initiated by remarks from mothers would tend to begin with requests, rather than provisions of information, and to end with minimal, rather than extended replies. It also suggested that conversational exchanges initiated by remarks from children would tend to begin with provisions, rather than requests for information, and to end with minimal, rather than extended replies. By the end of this chapter, it will be clear that these suggestions are not so much wrong as oversimplified.

During the first recordings, the percentages of mother-initiated exchanges ending with minimal rather than extended replies were always as high as expected. The same was true of the percentages of child-initiated exchanges beginning with provisions rather than requests for information. Contrary to expectation however, the percentages of mother-initiated exchanges beginning with requests rather than provisions of information, and child-initiated exchanges ending with minimal rather than extended replies were not always particularly high. The mother-initiated exchanges produced by five mother – child pairs virtually always began with provisions rather than requests for information. Their child-initiated exchanges frequently ended with extended rather than minimal replies. Another 11 mother – child pairs conformed to expectation in producing relatively high percentages of mother-initiated exchanges beginning with requests, rather than provisions of information. However, their child-initiated exchanges also frequently ended with extented rather than minimal replies. Only eight mother – child pairs produced high percentages of both mother-initiated exchanges beginning with requests, rather than provisions of information, and child-initiated exchanges ending with minimal, rather than extended, replies.

A. The pattern of mother-initiated exchanges

The analysis started by considering what have been called 'mother-initiated' exchanges, that is conversational exchanges beginning with remarks from the mothers. Before the percentages of requests, as opposed to provisions of information, and minimal, as opposed to extended, replies were computed, these exchanges were subjected to simple quantitative and qualitative analysis. Quantitative analysis revealed that during the first recording the 24 mother – child pairs produced between 3 and 53 mother-initiated exchanges ($M = 18.92$; SD $= 13.34$).[1] The low incidence of these exchanges could not be attributed to the frequency with which the mothers addressed remarks requesting or providing information to their children ($M = 115.17$; SD $= 74.51$). Rather, it seemed to reflect the low percentages of these remarks receiving replies from the children ($M = 18.14\%$; SD $= 9.30$). Qualitative analysis revealed that between 40 and 100 per cent ($M = 75.25\%$; SD $= 18.33$) of the exchanges that did occur began with remarks about names of objects, as in (3.1) and (3.2):

(3.1)   [Mother shows picture of boat to Philip (21:8)]
         Mother: What's this?
         Philip: Air. Air.

(3.2)   [Faye (21:16) pulls umbrella out of cupboard]
         Mother: That's the umbrella.
         Faye: Yes.

Between 0 and 50 per cent ($M = 8.67\%$; SD $= 13.50$) began with remarks about properties of objects, as in (3.3), and between 0 and 30 per cent ($M = 5.72\%$; SD $= 7.06$) began with remarks about names and properties of objects, as in (3.4):

   (3.3) [Mother directs Ian's (21:0) attention to another car]
          Mother: What colour's this one?
          Ian: Yellow.

   (3.4) [Mother and Nicola (20:19) look outside]
          Mother: Big lorry.
          Nicola: Lorry.

Although some mother-initiated exchanges began with remarks about quantities, owners, locations and actions of objects, these other kinds of information were not mentioned in this context more than 5 per cent of the time.

(a) Request or provision of information

Although this uniformity in the information mentioned raises interesting questions, they are not of central importance for the present discussion. Much more important is the question of how often the information was requested rather than provided by the mothers. Previous research had, of course, indicated that requests for information would occur quite frequently. To see whether that was the case, the percentages of mother-initiated exchanges beginning with requests and provisions of information were computed for every mother – child pair. As Table 3.1 shows, the percentages beginning with requests ranged from 0 to 83.33 per cent ($M = 44.13\%$; SD $= 22.49$). When these percentages are grouped at 10 per cent intervals in Fig. 3.1, a curious phenomenon emerges. Fig. 3.1 shows that the mother – child pairs seemed to fall into two distinct groups. One group of five pairs produced surprisingly low percentages of exchanges beginning with requests for information, but another group of 19 pairs produced the expected sizeable percentages.

This division could be caused by the mothers in the first group producing proportionately fewer requests for information during the first recording than the mothers in the second group. To check this possibility, the percentage of requests as opposed to provisions of information was computed for every mother. Overall, the mothers in the first group ($M = 20.93\%$; SD $= 11.81$) did produce proportionately fewer requests for information than the mothers in the second group ($M = 31.18\%$; SD $= 9.47$).

Table 3.1. *Percentage of mother-initiated exchanges beginning
with requests and provisions of information*

Name	Requests information	Provides information	Total
Alan	4 (19.05%)	17 (80.95%)	21
Barry	17 (48.57%)	18 (51.43%)	35
Caroline	0 (0%)	6 (100.00%)	6
Daniel	6 (42.86%)	8 (57.14%)	14
Eileen	5 (83.33%)	1 (16.67%)	6
Faye	4 (80.00%)	1 (20.00%)	5
Graham	3 (35.71%)	9 (64.29%)	14
Hayley	6 (54.55%)	5 (45.45%)	11
Ian	12 (60.00%)	8 (40.00%)	20
Jason	2 (40.00%)	3 (60.00%)	5
Kevin	24 (45.28%)	29 (54.72%)	53
Lucy	1 (33.33%)	2 (66.67%)	3
Melanie	2 (33.33%)	4 (66.67%)	6
Nicola	4 (33.33%)	8 (66.67%)	12
Oliver	8 (19.05%)	34 (80.95%)	42
Philip	12 (50.00%)	12 (50.00%)	24
Richard	0 (0%)	21 (100.00%)	21
Sally	20 (58.82%)	14 (41.18%)	34
Tom	7 (63.64%)	4 (36.36%)	11
Ursula	25 (73.53%)	9 (26.47%)	34
Virginia	11 (47.83%)	12 (52.17%)	23
Wayne	4 (16.00%)	21 (84.00%)	25
Yvonne	14 (58.33%)	10 (41.67%)	24
Zoe	5 (62.50%)	3 (37.50%)	8

Analysis by t-test showed that this difference was almost significant ($t = 2.05$ df $= 22$; $p \simeq 0.05$). In addition however, the division could be caused by the children in the first group replying to proportionately fewer requests and/or proportionately more provisions during the first recording than the children in the second group. To check this possibility, the percentages of maternal requests and maternal provisions receiving replies in the first recording were computed for every child. Analysis by t-test revealed that the children in the first group ($M = 8.02\%$; SD $= 8.63$) did reply to significantly fewer requests for information ($t = 2.48$; df $= 22$; $p < 0.05$) than the children in the second group ($M = 33.31\%$; SD $= 22.02$). Moreover, the children in the first group ($M = 23.84\%$; SD $= 10.63$) almost replied to significantly more provisions of information ($t = 1.86$; df $= 22$; Not significant) than the children in the second group ($M = 13.11\%$; SD $= 11.67$). Thus, the unexpected division in Fig. 3.1 was created partly by differences in the percentages of requests for information produced by the mothers, and partly by differences in the percentages of requests and provisions of information receiving replies from the children.

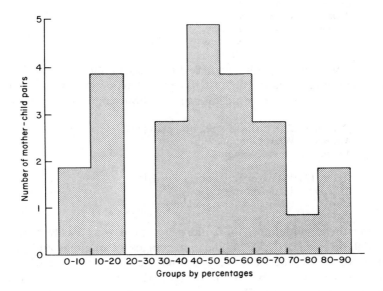

Figure 3.1: *Grouping of mother–child pairs by percentage of mother-initiated-exchanges beginning with requests for information*

(b) Minimal or extended replies

Having looked at the percentages of requests, as opposed to provisions of information in mother-initiated exchanges, it is appropriate to consider the percentages of extended, as opposed to minimal, replies. It will be remembered that replies were regarded as minimal if they provided requested information, as in (3.5), or if they gave evaluative and/or corrective feedback on provided information, as in (3.6) and (3.7):

(3.5) [Mother shows model animal to Tom (21:3)]
    Mother: What's this?
    Tom: Monkey.

(3.6) [Mother indicates doll to Caroline (21:3)]
    Mother: There's your dolly.
    Caroline: Dolly.

(3.7) [Daniel (20:13) holds model animal]
    Mother: It's a kangaroo.
    Daniel: Camel.
    Mother: Kangaroo.
    Daniel: Cows. Cows. Cows. Cows.
    Mother: It's a kangaroo.
    Daniel: Cow. No. No, cow.
              No, cow. No, cow.

On the other hand, replies were regarded as extended if they fulfilled the minimal requirements and requested or provided new information about the same subject, as in (3.8), or old information about a new subject, as in (3.9):

(3.8) [Yvonne (22:0) pushes piece into jigsaw]
    Mother: What's that one?
    Yvonne: Onion. Naughty.

(3.9) [Barry (21:18) plays with model animals]
    Mother: ' That's one bear.
    Barry: Uhm, and here another bear.

Using these guidelines, the children's replies were easily classified as minimal or extended. Then, the percentages of minimal and extended replies were computed for every mother – child pair to see whether the predominance of minimal replies suggested by earlier research occurred with the present sample. The percentages are presented in Table 3.2, which shows that the percentages of extended replies were sometimes as low as 0 per cent and never rose above 28.57 per cent (M = 8.01%; SD = 9.15). When these percentages are grouped at 3 per cent intervals[2] in Fig. 3.2, it becomes even more apparent that extended replies were generally very infrequent. However, without forming a distinct group, some children did produce considerably more extended replies than others. The significance of this variability will soon become clear.

Closer inspection of the ubiquitous minimal replies revealed some other interesting, if less central, features. Firstly, the vast majority of minimal replies to remarks that provided information were evaluative (M = 91.60%; SD = 17.32), rather than corrective. Presumably, small children rarely challenge the authority of their mothers. Secondly, the vast majority of evaluative remarks used imitation (M = 87.51%; SD = 19.87), as in (3.10), rather than some other conventional term, as in (3.11):

(3.10) [Ursula (21:3) sits in bowl]
    Mother: Ursula's sitting in the bowl.
    Ursula: Bowl.
              Bowl.

Table 3.2. *Percentage of mother-initiated exchanges ending with minimal and extended replies*

Name	Minimal reply	Extended reply	Total
Alan	18 (85.71%)	3 (14.29%)	21
Barry	25 (71.43%)	10 (28.57%)	35
Caroline	6 (100.00%)	0 (0%)	6
Daniel	14 (100.00%)	0 (0%)	14
Eileen	6 (100.00%)	0 (0%)	6
Faye	5 (100.00%)	0 (0%)	5
Graham	14 (100.00%)	0 (0%)	14
Hayley	10 (90.91%)	1 (9.09%)	11
Ian	20 (100.00%)	0 (0%)	20
Jason	5 (100.00%)	0 (0%)	5
Kevin	41 (77.36%)	12 (22.64%)	53
Lucy	3 (100.00%)	0 (0%)	3
Melanie	6 (100.00%)	0 (0%)	6
Nicola	10 (83.33%)	2 (16.67%)	12
Oliver	39 (92.86%)	3 (7.14%)	42
Philip	23 (95.83%)	1 (4.17%)	24
Richard	21 (100.00%)	0 (0%)	21
Sally	32 (94.12%)	2 (5.88%)	34
Tom	10 (90.91%)	1 (9.09%)	11
Ursula	34 (100.00%)	0 (0%)	34
Virginia	19 (82.61%)	4 (17.39%)	23
Wayne	19 (76.00%)	6 (24.00%)	25
Yvonne	19 (79.17%)	5 (20.83%)	24
Zoe	7 (87.50%)	1 (12.50%)	8

(3.11) [Mother shows crayon to Ian (21:0)]
    Mother: That's a blue one.
    Ian: Yes.

Despite the overall popularity of imitation, it should be pointed out that two children showed a distinct preference for other forms of evaluation. The existence of these children is rather interesting in view of Ryan's (1973) summary of imitation research. As Ryan pointed out, this research suggested that, at any given age level, children vary considerably in their propensity to imitate. Apparently, some children never imitate, whereas others imitate over half of the time. Such variations can be partially attributed to differences across studies in definitions of imitation. However, variations appeared within studies when imitation was obviously assessed by the same criteria. The present research suggests that within-study variations may be partially due to some children using imitation to give evaluative replies and others using non-imitative forms.

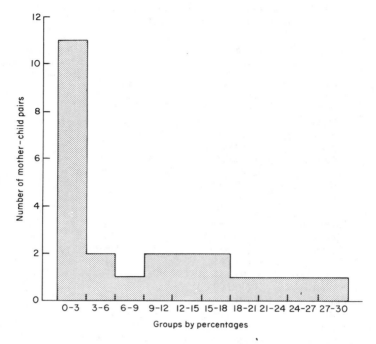

Figure 3.2. *Grouping of mother–child pairs by percentage of mother-initiated-exchanges ending with extended replies*

B. The pattern of child-initiated exchanges

Perhaps the most obvious difference between conversational exchanges beginning with remarks from the mothers, and conversational exchanges beginning with remarks from the children, was in terms of frequency. During the first recording, the 24 mother – child pairs produced between 5 and 95 conversational exchanges ($M = 35.29$; SD $= 21.79$) beginning with remarks from the children. Thus, these 'child-initiated' exchanges were on average approximately twice as frequent as mother-initiated exchanges, a difference that proved to be significant on a matched-pairs t-test ($t = 6.43$; df $= 23$; $p < 0.001$). Further analysis by matched-pairs t-test showed that the difference could not be explained by the children addressing more remarks that requested or provided information ($M = 148.33$; SD $= 77.84$) than their mothers ($t = 1.67$; df $= 23$; Not significant). Rather, it was due to the mothers replying proportionately more often ($M = 24.67\%$; SD $= 12.03$) than their children ($t = 2.64$; df $= 23$; $p < 0.02$). Although child-initiated exchanges were more frequent than mother-initiated exchanges, they seemed, if anything, less varied in informational content. Between 57.5 and 100 per cent (M = 82.84%; SD = 11.58) began with remarks about names of objects, and between 0 and 26.32 per cent (M = 7.75%; SD = 7.76) began with remarks about properties of objects. It was sometimes rather difficult to classify the informational content of the remaining remarks. For example, certain nouns might have been declaring the owner, recipient or location of given objects. The clear examples of these topics never amounted to more than 5 per cent of the child-initiated exchanges.

(a) Request or provision of information

Again however, the main focus was not frequency and content, but form. Specifically, the focus was on the percentages of exchanges beginning with requests, as opposed to provisions of information. Looking at these percentages in Table 3.3, it is clear that expectations derived from earlier studies were overwhelmingly confirmed. Very few child-initiated exchanges began with requests for information. In fact, exchanges beginning with requests provided only 0–26.47 per cent of the total (M = 4.44%; SD = 7.84). When the percentages are arranged at 3 per cent intervals in Fig. 3.3, their distribution at the lower end of this already limited range becomes even clearer.

In theory, the low percentages of child-initiated exchanges beginning with requests for information could have resulted from the children producing percentages of requests that were low in comparison with their percentages of provisions. Alternatively, it could have resulted from the percentages of requests receiving replies being low relative to the percentages of provisions. In fact, the first explanation seemed most likely. The percentages of requests produced by the children were generally low in the first recording (M = 4.30%; SD = 5.10). However, the percentages of requests receiving replies from the mothers (M = 19.00%; SD = 24.75) were no different (t = 0.79; df^3 = 18; Not significant) from the percentages of provisions (M = 23.66%; SD = 14.59).

(b) Minimal or extended replies

Having seen that, with few exceptions, the percentages of child-initiated exchanges beginning with requests almost always reached the expected low level, the next step was to see whether the percentages of child-initiated exchanges ending with extended replies were also as low as expected. As with the children, the mothers' replies were regarded as minimal if they provided requested information or gave evaluative and/or corrective feedback on provided information. As with the children, evaluative feedback

Table 3.3. *Percentage of child-initiated exchanges beginning with requests and provisions of information*

Name	Requests information	Provides information	Total
Alan	0(0%)	26 (100.00%)	26
Barry	0 (0%)	37 (100.00%)	37
Caroline	0 (0%)	15 (100.00%)	15
Daniel	2 (4.65%)	51 (95.35%)	43
Eileen	0 (0%)	5 (100.00%)	5
Faye	1 (16.67%)	5 (83.33%)	6
Graham	6 (12.00%)	44 (88.00%)	50
Hayley	0 (0%)	32 (100.00%)	32
Ian	1 (1.79%)	55 (98.21%)	56
Jason	2 (25.00%)	6 (75.00%)	8
Kevin	0 (0%)	99 (100.00%)	99
Lucy	0 (0%)	5 (100.00%)	5
Melanie	0 (0%)	16 (100.00%)	16
Nicola	0 (0%)	20 (100.00%)	20
Oliver	0 (0%)	54 (100.00%)	54
Philip	4 (9.52%)	38 (90.48%)	42
Richard	3 (10.00%)	27 (90.00%)	30
Sally	3 (5.17%)	55 (94.83%)	58
Tom	0 (0%)	24 (100.00%)	24
Ursula	0 (0%)	46 (100.00%)	46
Virginia	0 (0%)	45 (100.00%)	45
Wayne	0 (0%)	48 (100.00%)	48
Yvonne	0 (0%)	48 (100.00%)	48
Zoe	9 (26.47%)	25 (73.53%)	34

predominated ($M = 83.54\%$; $SD = 11.22$) in the minimal replies mothers gave to provided information. This was in spite of the mothers correcting, not only because they regarded the provided information as wrong, as in (3.12), but also because they regarded the provided information as too general, as in (3.13):

(3.12) [Yvonne (22:0) looks at me]
      Yvonne: Girl.
      Mother: It's a lady.
                Not girl.
                Not girl when you don't know them.

(3.13) [Daniel (20:13) plays with model animals]
      Daniel: Bird.
      Mother: Uhm, bird.
                It's a penguin.

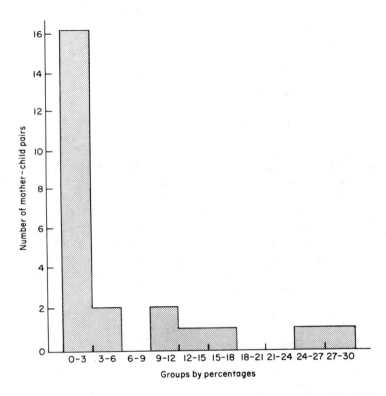

Figure 3.3: *Grouping of mother-child pairs by percentage of mother-initiated-exchanges beginning with requests for information.*

Chapter 1 pointed out that there has been a considerable amount of research into the incidence and implications of maternal 'expansion'. It will be remembered that expansion involves incorporating children's remarks into well formed sentences, as in (3.14):

(3.14) [Eileen (22:9) finds Dougall]
   Eileen: Baby.
       Bow-wow.
   Mother: That's a bow-wow, isn't it?

To estimate the incidence of expansion in the present study, well formed sentences that occurred in isolation, such as the mother's reply in (3.14), and well formed sentences that occurred with other evaluative expressions, such as the mother's reply in (3.15), were counted as expansions:

(3.15) [Kevin (20:21) looks at picture]
    Kevin: Fork.
    Mother: Uhm.
             What is it?
             Fork?
             Yes, it's a fork, isn't it?

Given this definition of expansion, it was clear that the mothers varied greatly in the extent to which they used expansion to express positive feedback. Expansions actually accounted for between 0 and 100 per cent ($M = 20.99\%$; SD = 22.21) of those replies from the mothers that expressed positive feedback. This individual variation seems even greater than that mentioned by Slobin (1968) in his review of related research.

Several interesting features also emerged from consideration of extended replies, that is replies that requested or provided new information about the same subject or old information about a new subject, in addition to fulfilling the aforementioned minimal requirements. It was pointed out in Chapter 1 that extensions can be embedded in minimal replies, as in (3.16), or kept quite separate from them, as in (3.17):

(3.16) [Graham (20:19) holds model animal]
    Graham: Elly. Elly. Elly.
    Mother: That's a big elephant.

(3.17) [Zoe (21:4) looks at picture on block]
    Zoe: Dice.
    Mother: That's a kite.
             It goes up in the air.
             It's a kite.

Although embedded extensions have a ring of artificiality to adult speakers of English, they were quite frequent in the mothers' speech. They accounted for between 0 and 100 per cent ($M = 45.53\%$; SD = 29.80) of the extended replies produced by the 20 mothers who gave some extended replies at all.

However, calculating the percentages of extended replies as opposed to minimal replies yielded the most interesting results of all. As Table 3.4 shows, these percentages were not always particularly low. In fact, between 0 and 41.41 per cent ($M = 21.34\%$; SD = 13.19) of total replies were extended. Moreover, once these percentages were grouped at 5 per cent intervals, as in Fig. 3.4, it was clear that they were not normally distributed across the range. Instead, the mother – child pairs seemed to fall into two

Table 3.4. *Percentage of child-initiated exchanges ending with minimal and extended replies*

Name	Minimal reply	Extended reply	Total
Alan	16 (61.54%)	10 (38.46%)	26
Barry	29 (78.38%)	8 (21.62%)	37
Caroline	9 (60.00%)	6 (40.00%)	15
Daniel	33 (76.74%)	10 (23.26%)	43
Eileen	5 (100.00%)	0 (0%)	5
Faye	6 (100.00%)	0 (0%)	6
Graham	40 (80.00%)	10 (20.00%)	50
Hayley	29 (90.62%)	3 (9.38%)	32
Ian	48 (85.71%)	8 (14.29%)	56
Jason	7 (87.50%)	1 (12.50%)	8
Kevin	58 (58.59%)	41 (41.41%)	99
Lucy	5 (100.00%)	0 (0%)	5
Melanie	16 (100.00%)	0 (0%)	16
Nicola	15 (75.00%)	5 (25.00%)	20
Oliver	36 (66.67%)	18 (33.33%)	54
Philip	41 (97.62%)	1 (2.38%)	42
Richard	21 (70.00%)	9 (30.00%)	30
Sally	44 (75.86%)	14 (24.14%)	58
Tom	16 (66.67%)	8 (33.33%)	24
Ursula	32 (69.57%)	14 (30.43%)	46
Virginia	33 (73.33%)	12 (26.67%)	45
Wayne	34 (70.83%)	14 (29.17%)	48
Yvonne	33 (68.75%)	15 (31.25%)	48
Zoe	26 (76.47%)	8 (25.53%)	34

distinct groups. One group of eight pairs conformed to expectation and produced extremely low percentages of child-initiated exchanges ending with extended replies. However, another group of 16 pairs produced quite sizeable percentages of child-initiated exchanges ending with extended replies.

C. The overall pattern of mother–child conversation

The two groups that emerged from considering child-initiated exchanges ending with extended replies are reminiscent of the two groups that emerged from considering mother-initiated exchanges beginning with requests for information. However, none of the mothers and children fell into *both* the group producing low percentages of child-initiated exchanges ending with extended replies *and* the group producing low percentages of mother-initiated exchanges beginning with requests for information. In other words, they fell into three groups:

1. One group of five pairs who produced low percentages of mother-initiated exchanges beginning with requests and moderate percentages of child-initiated exchanges ending with extended replies.
2. One group of eight pairs who produced high percentages of mother initiated exchanges beginning with requests and low percentages of child-initiated exchanges ending with extended replies.
2. One group of 11 pairs who produced high percentages of mother-initiated exchanges beginning with requests and moderate percentages of child-initiated exchanges ending with extended replies.

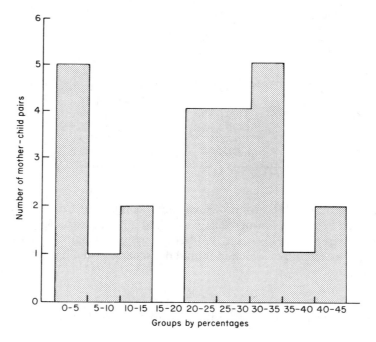

Figure 3.4: *Grouping of mother – child pairs by percentage of child-initiated exchanges ending with extended replies.*

All three groups produced extremely low percentages of mother-initiated exchanges ending with extended replies and child-initiated exchanges beginning with requests for information. Thus, the overall characteristics of the groups can be summarized as in Table 3.5.

Table 3.5. *Overall characteristics of the groups*

	Mother-initiated		Child-initiated	
Number of pairs	% Beginning with requests	% Ending with extended	% Beginning with requests	% Ending with extended
5	Low	Low	Low	Moderate
8	High	Low	Low	Low
11	High	Low	Low	Moderate

Looking at the first group, it will be apparent that most of their mother-initiated exchanges must have begun with provisions of information and ended with minimal replies, as in (3.18):

(1.38) [Richard (21:21) looks at video-camera]
    Mother: Camera.
    Richard: Cam'.

Most of their child-initiated exchanges must have begun with provisions of information. However, some must have ended with minimal replies, as in (3.19), and some with extended replies, as in (3.20):

(3.19) [Oliver (20:10) picks up model tigers]
    Oliver: Lions.
    Mother: Lions, are they?

(3.20) [Caroline (21:3) tips doll upside down]
    Caroline: Dolly not nap on.
             No nap on.
    Mother: No, but she's got some pretty pants on.

Previous analysis showed that maternal requests were rare in the first group. Hence exchanges where the mothers gave extended replies must have contained provisions of information, as in (3.20), rather than requests for information, as in (3.21):

(3.21) [Daniel (20:13) cuddles toy cat]
    Daniel: That pussy
    Mother: That's pussy.
             Where shall we put pussy?

Of course, the exchanges that characterized the first group did not always occur in isolation. Sometimes, they occurred in sequences such that the final remark in a mother-initiated exchange became the first remark in a child-initiated exchange. Given the particular exchanges produced by the first group, these sequences could take one of two forms. They could take the form illustrated by (3.22), where a minimal reply from the mother that provides information elicits a minimal reply from the child *ad infinitum*:

(3.22) [Caroline (21:3) discovers doll's clothes]
    Caroline: Look, hat.
    Mother: A hat.
    Caroline: Hat.
    Mother: Hat.
    Caroline: Hat.
    Mother: Hat.

Alternatively, they could take the form illustrated by (3.23), where an extended reply from the mother that provides information elicits a minimal reply from the child, again *ad infinitum*:

(3.23) [Alan (22:9) looks outside]
    Alan: Wind.
    Mother: Can you hear the wind?
    Alan: Wind.
    Mother: Yes, the wind's blowing the fence.
    Alan: Wind.
    Mother: Wind going whoosh.

Of course, they could, like (3.24), take some combination of the forms illustrated by (3.22) and (3.23):

(3.24) [Nicola (20:19) discovers model fireman]
    Nicola: Man.
    Mother: Man, isn't he nice!
    Nicola: Man.
    Mother: Man, uhm.
    Nicola: Man.
    Mother: Yes, has he got a hat on?

Clearly, none of these sequences constitutes what adults would regard as discourse. The essence of discourse is the addition of new information in a step-by-step fashion. In (3.22) nothing is added beyond the original piece of information. Rather, this information is repeated over and over. (3.23) comes somewhat closer, insofar as the mother did add something new during her turn to speak. However, the child's insistence on repeating his original contribution precluded a steady movement forwards. Instead, it forced the conversation to keep returning to its starting place, creating the impression that the mother was making a few hesitant excursions from a home-base provided by the child. On further reflection, the 'excursive' analogy might provide a useful framework for thinking about the first group. This is partly because it labels their best performances and partly because it contrasts phonologically with the 'discursive' conversations they failed to create. Hence from now onwards, the first group will be referred to as the 'excursive group'.

If the best efforts of the first group took the form of excursions, the second group achieved even less. From Table 3.5 it will be clear that this group engaged in two types of mother-initiated exchange. These were mother-initiated exchanges beginning with requests for information and ending with minimal replies, and mother-initiated exchanges beginning with provisions of information and ending with minimal replies. The two types of exchange are illustrated in (3.25) and (3.26), respectively:

(3.25) [Yvonne (22:0) discovers doll's bottle]
  Mother: What's that?
  Yvonne: It's a Mummy.

(3.26) [Sally (20:8) points to my multi-coloured shoes and says 'Okay shoes']
  Mother: They're nice, aren't they?
  Sally: Nice.

However, virtually all child-initiated exchanges produced by the second group began with provisions of information and ended with minimal replies, as in (3.27):

(3.27) [Hayley (20:11) discovers model elephant]
  Hayley: Elenute. Elenute.
  Mother: Uhm.

Frequently, the second group produced sequences of mother-initiated exchanges beginning with requests followed by child-initiated exchanges ending with minimal replies. Sometimes, several of these two-exchange conversations would occur in quick succession, as in (3.28):

(3.28) [Mother shows model animal to Philip (21:8)]
  Mother: What's that?
  Philip: Doggie.
  Mother: That's not a doggie; that's a lion.
      And what's that?
  Philip: Doggie.
  Mother: Penguin.

On other occasions, the second group produced strings of exchanges that began with provisions of information and ended with minimal replies. (3.22) contained one example of these strings; (3.29) contains another:

(3.29) [Jason (20:16) builds jigsaw]
    Jason: Cock.
    Mother: Cock.
    Jason: Cock.
    Mother: Cock.
    Jason: Cock.

In (3.28) a simple sequence recycles several times. In (3.29) one piece of information is repeated *ad nauseam*. For both reasons (and once more to contrast with the 'discursive' conversations they manifestly failed to produce), it seems appropriate to label the second group as the 'recursive group'.

Unlike the excursive and recursive groups, the third group produced two types of mother-initiated exchange *and* two types of child-initiated exchange. As Table 3.5 showed, their mother-initiated exchanges usually ended with minimal replies. However, they began with both requests for information, as in (3.30), and provisions of information, as in (3.31):

(3.30) [Mother shows Ursula (21:3) picture on brick]
    Mother: What's that, Ursula?
    Mother: Brick.

(3.31) [Mother and Nicola (20:19) gaze at dead bird]
    Mother: It looked too big to fall out.
    Nicola: Ah fall out.
             Out.

The child-initiated exchanges produced by the third group generally began with provisions of information. They ended with both minimal replies, as in (3.32), and extended replies, as in (3.33):

(3.32) [Wayne (20:4) hits nose with cardboard tube]
    Wayne: A bang.
    Mother: A bang, wasn't it?

(3.33) [Kevin (20:21) gives coffee cup to mother]
    Kevin: Oh coffee, coffee, coffee.
    Mother: Is that coffee?
             Coffee from the teapot?

Unlike the excursive group, maternal extensions often took the form of requests for information, as in (3.34):

(3.34) [Mother shows picture to Tom (21:3)]
    Tom: Baby duck.
    Mother: That's a big duck.
             That's a Mummy duck.
             What's she doing, look?

Sometimes, remarks like the mothers' contribution to (3.34) received replies. This produced sequences of child-initiated exchanges ending with extended replies, followed by mother-initiated exchanges beginning with requests for information. (3.35) and (3.36) contain examples of such sequences:

(3.35) [Mother shows model chimp to Virginia (21:17)]
    Mother: What's this?
    Virginia: Monkey.
    Mother: A huge monkey.
             A huge monkey.
             And what does he say?
             Eh, what does he say?
    Virginia: Eh-eh. Eh-eh.

(3.36) [Ursula (21:3) looks at pictures on brick]
    Mother: What's this then?
    Ursula: Parrot.
    Mother: Parrot, yes.
             What's parrot doing?
    Ursula: Squawk-squawk-squawk.

In (3.35) and (3.36), there are some signs of genuine discourse. In other words, new information about a given subject is being gradually accumulated. Of course, information is being amassed less efficiently and more deliberately than it would be in ordinary adult conversation. Nevertheless, the discursive elements are undeniable. Having said this, it must be pointed out that the mothers and children in the third group also held conversations like the mothers and children in the excursive and recursive groups. This was inevitable given their overlapping characteristics. However to mark their relative approximation to true discourse through those exchanges which were unique to themselves, they will now be called the 'discursive group'.

The three groups that have now been labelled 'excursive', 'recursive' and 'discursive' emerged after consideration of exchanges that occurred with noticeable frequency. Specifically, the groups were deemed to produce exchanges that occurred with at least 'moderate' frequency. Group differences were presumed when exchanges occurred with at least moderate

Table 3.6. *Comparison of mother – child groups*

Mother-initiated exchanges

Group	Percentage beginning with requests		Percentage ending with extended replies	
	M	SD	*M*	SD
Excursive (E)	10.82%	9.96	9.09%	10.23
Recursive (R)	54.32%	19.41	1.66%	3.34
Discursive (D)	51.85%	12.52	12.14%	9.97

$t_{E \text{ v } R} = 4.59$; df $= 11$; $p < 0.001$
$t_{E \text{ v } D} = 6.42$; df $= 14$; $p < 0.001$
$t_{R \text{ v } D} = 0.34$; df $= 17$; Not sig

$t_{E \text{ v } R} = 1.94$; df $= 11$; Not sig
$t_{E \text{ v } D} = 0.56$; df $= 14$; Not sig
$t_{R \text{ v } D} = 2.84$; df $= 17$; $p < 0.02$

Child-initiated exchanges

Group	Percentage beginning with requests		Percentage ending with extended replies	
	M	SD	*M*	SD
Excursive (E)	2.00%	4.47	34.19%	4.89
Recursive (R)	6.62%	9.61	4.82%	6.19
Discursive (D)	4.39%	8.25	27.51%	6.17

$t_{E \text{ v } R} = 8.96$; df $= 11$; $p < 0.001$
$t_{E \text{ v } D} = 2.12$; df $= 14$; Not sig
$t_{R \text{ v } D} = 7.90$; df $= 17$; $p < 0.001$

frequency in one group and below moderate frequency in another. Although this kind of analysis helps to characterize the groups, it must be supplemented by finer investigation. It does not show the exact magnitude of the categorical differences, nor does it reveal whether the groups differed in exchanges that they produced with globally similar frequencies. To investigate these issues, the mean and standard deviation percentages of mother-initiated exchanges beginning with requests for information and ending with extended replies, and child-initiated exchanges beginning with requests for information and ending with extended replies were computed for each group. Table 3.6 presents the figures. One-way analyses of variance revealed significant differences between the groups in the percentages of mother-initiated exchanges beginning with requests for information ($F = 16.05$; df $= 2/21$; $p < 0.001$), the percentages of mother-initiated exchanges ending with extended replies ($F = 3.64$; df $= 2/21$; $p < 0.05$) and the percentages of child-initiated exchanges ending with extended replies ($F = 48.33$; df $= 2/21$; $p < 0.001$). There were no significant group differences in the percentages of child-initiated exchanges beginning with requests for information ($F = 0.50$; df $= 2/21$; Not significant). The group means were compared on t-tests to clarify the differences that were significant, and the results of this comparison are also shown in Table 3.6. Comparing the mean percentages of mother-initiated exchanges beginning with requests for information revealed that the excursive group produced significantly fewer of these exchanges than the recursive and discursive groups, who did not differ significantly from each other. Comparing the mean percentages of child-initiated exchanges ending with extended replies revealed that the recursive group produced significantly fewer of these exchanges than the excursive and discursive groups, who did not differ significantly from each other. These results simply show that the differences on which the groups were based reached statistical significance. Comparing the mean percentages of mother-initiated exchanges ending with extended replies produced more surprising results. The recursive group produced significantly fewer of these exchanges than the discursive group, and nearly produced fewer than the excursive group. However, the recursive group consisted of the mother – child pairs who produced very few child-initiated exchanges ending with extended replies. Thus, it seems that the pattern of replies produced by the mothers was reproduced to some extent by their children.

The existence of the groups means that the picture of early conversation painted from previous research must have been too simple. The essence of that picture was uniformity at given age levels, but the discovery of three groups bears witness to considerable variability. However, despite its excessive simplicity, the picture of early conversation was by no means entirely wrong. Firstly, it suggested that a high percentage of mother-initiated exchanges should begin with requests rather than provisions of information. Over half of the mother-initiated exchanges produced by the recursive and discursive groups did begin with requests for information. Only the excursive group failed to produce high percentages of mother-initiated exchanges beginning with requests. Secondly, the picture suggested that a high percentage of mother-initiated exchanges should end with minimal rather than extended replies. Despite the difference documented in the previous paragraph, none of the groups used mother-initiated exchanges ending with extended replies more than 12 per cent of the time. Thirdly, the original picture of early conversation indicated that a high percentage of child-initiated exchanges should begin with provisions rather than requests for information. No group produced child-initiated exchanges beginning with requests for information more than 6 per cent of the time. Finally, the picture suggested that a high percentage of child-initiated exchanges should end with minimal rather than extended replies. Although about 30 per cent of the child-initiated exchanges produced by the excursive and discursive groups ended with extended replies, the recursive group did conform to expectation. In the recursive group, less than 5 per cent of child-initiated exchanges ended with extended replies.

In fact, the recursive group concurred with the original picture of mother – child conversation in every respect. The discursive group differed in child-initiated exchanges ending with minimal replies, but concurred in every other respect. The excursive group differed in child-initiated exchanges ending with minimal replies and mother-initiated exchanges beginning with requests for information, but concurred in the other two respects. In other words, the pattern of conversation produced by the present mothers and children varied from complete to partial concurrence with the picture painted from earlier studies. Faced with this conclusion, it is tempting to ask whether the same was true for subsequent changes in the pattern of mother – child conversation. Chapter 1 made several suggestions about these subsequent changes. Perhaps the extent to which they occurred varied across mothers and children. Perhaps it was dependent on the original pattern of mother – child conversation. Perhaps the situation was altogether more complex. The next chapter will consider the conversations held by the three groups in the second recording with a view to exploring these possibilities. Since its conclusions will be incomprehensible without a clear understanding of the differences between these groups in the first recording, this chapter will end with fairly lengthy extracts from the first-recording conversations held by representatives of each group. The differences between the groups should become more intuitively 'real' if these extracts are not simply read as text but also analysed using the criteria employed in this chapter. This means calculating the frequencies of the different exchanges and seeing why the inter-group variations produced sequences that suggested the terms 'excursive', 'recursive' and 'discursive'.

D. Extract from the first recording of an excursive mother – child pair

[Wayne (20:4) picks lorry up]
Wayne: Car.
Mother: Car, yes.
[Wayne picks front of lorry up]

Wayne: A door.
Mother: And a door.
Wayne: A door. A door.
Mother: Is that a door for the car?
Wayne: A door.
Mother: That's it, I think.
             Does it go on?
Wayne: Door.
Mother: Does the door go on?
             It's like your tip-up.
[Wayne puts front on lorry]
Wayne: A doodle-doo.
Mother: All doodle-doos on top.
[Wayne fingers wheels of lorry]
Wayne: Wee-wee.
Mother: That's it.
             How nice!
Wayne: A wee-wee. A wee-wee.
             A doodle-doo.
Mother: They're wheels, aren't they?
Wayne: Doodle-doo.
Mother: Wheels.

E. Extract from the first recording of a recursive mother – child pair

[Ian (21:0) looks at yellow car]
Mother: What colour's that one?
Ian: Colour it? Red.
Mother: It's a yellow one.
Ian: Yellow.
Mother: What colour's this one?
Ian: Yellow.
Mother: That's a yellow one, yes.
[Ian pushes red car]
Mother: What colour's that one?
Ian: Yellow.
Mother: That's red.
Ian: That yellow.
Mother: That's red.
Ian: So that.
[Ian hits another red car]
Ian: That red.
Mother: That's red.
Ian: No, that red.
[Ian touches yellow car]
Mother: That's yellow.
             What colour is this one?
[Mother points to blue car]

Ian: Colour is that? Colour that?
                That colour. No colour.
Mother: It's blue.

F. Extract from the first recording of a discursive mother–child pair

[Kevin (20:21) and mother look at picture book]
Mother: What's this?
Kevin: Phone.
Mother: Telephone.
                And who do we speak to on the telephone?
Kevin: Grandma.
Mother: Grandma, that's right.
Kevin: Tree.
Mother: Uhm, where's the tree in our garden?
[Kevin looks out of the window]
Kevin: There.
Mother: That's another tree, isn't it?
[Mother turns page]
Mother: What's that?
Kevin: Dumplings.
Mother: Dumplings, yes. Lovely.
Kevin: Duck.
Mother: Duck, yes.
                And what does the duck say?
Kevin: Duck.
Mother: Quack-quack-quack.
[Mother turns page]
Kevin: Duck, look.
Mother: Uhm? That's a swing.
                You like swinging, don't you?
                Swing–swing.

Notes

[1]*M* = Mean; SD = Standard Deviation
[2]The magnitude of the intervals used for grouping in the Figures reflects the magnitude of the range of values found in the Tables.
[3]The computation was based on 20 mother – child pairs because four children never requested information.

4 Conversational Exchanges in the Second Recording

Analysis of the conversational exchanges that occurred in the first recording revealed a certain amount of deviance from the pattern of mother–child conversation suggested by existing research. This research had suggested that mother-initiated exchanges should frequently begin with requests rather than provisions of information, and end with minimal rather than extended replies. Child-initiated exchanges should frequently begin with provisions rather than requests for information, and end with minimal rather than extended replies. Although the mother-initiated exchanges produced by the recursive and discursive groups did frequently begin with requests for information, the mother-initiated exchanges produced by the excursive group rarely did this. Although the child-initiated exchanges produced by the recursive group nearly always ended with minimal replies, the child-initiated exchanges produced by the excursive and discursive groups often ended with extended replies. However, all three groups conformed to expectation by producing mother-initiated exchanges that normally ended with minimal replies and child-initiated exchanges that normally began with provisions of information.

Given this situation, it seems rather unlikely that the conversational exchanges that occur in the second recording will yield all the changes over time mentioned in Chapter 1. Using earlier studies, Chapter 1 suggested that mother-initiated exchanges might increasingly begin with provisions rather than requests for information and end with extended rather than minimal replies. Child-initiated exchanges might increasingly begin with requests rather than provisions of information, and end with extended rather than minimal replies. Since mother-initiated exchanges beginning with provisions of information predominated in the excursive group during the first recording, it is hard to imagine them increasing still further by the second recording. Since child-initiated exchanges ending with extended replies were quite frequent in the excursive and discursive groups, but virtually unknown in the recursive group, it is equally hard to imagine them increasing in any straightforward manner by the second recording. On the other hand, all three groups left plenty of scope for the hypothesized increases in mother-initiated exchanges ending with extended replies and child-initiated exchanges beginning with requests for information.

Bearing all this in mind, this chapter will analyse the conversational exchanges that occurred in the second recording to see exactly what did happen. It will report a complex situation that had two broad undercurrents. Firstly, the group differences were reduced, but by no means eliminated, by the second recording. Specifically, the percentages of mother-initiated exchanges beginning with requests for information increased for the excursive group, and decreased for the recursive and discursive groups to narrow the gap quite considerably. The percentages of child-initiated exchanges ending with extended replies increased for the recursive group and remained fairly constant for the excursive and discursive groups, again narrowing the gap to some considerable extent. Secondly, any changes in the percentages of those exchanges that had not been strongly group-differentiated in the first recording were in the suggested direction. In particular, the percentages of mother-initiated exchanges ending with extended replies increased for the recursive group and remained fairly stable for the excursive and discursive groups. The percentages of child-initiated exchanges beginning with requests for information increased slightly for all three groups.

A. The changes in mother-initiated exchanges

As before, the analysis began by considering conversational exchanges that started with contributions from the mothers. The 24 mother – child pairs produced between 3 and 123 of these mother-initiated exchanges ($M = 47.92$; $SD = 30.05$) during the second recording. Analysis by matched-pairs t-test revealed that this was significantly more than during the first recording ($t = 4.70$; df $= 23$; $p < 0.001$). This was partly because the mothers addressed their children with more requests and provisions of information ($M = 167.79$; $SD = 83.62$) during the second recording ($t = 3.01$; df $= 23$; $p < 0.01$). It was also because the children replied to a greater percentage of these requests and provisions of information ($M = 28.19\%$; $SD = 9.66$) during the second recording ($t = 3.44$; df $= 23$; $p < 0.01$).

Moreover, mother-initiated exchanges not only increased in frequency, but also became more varied in informational content. It was true that the percentages of these exchanges ($M = 8.29\%$; $SD = 9.90$) beginning with remarks about properties of objects remained fairly constant ($t = 0.11$; df $=$

23; Not significant) across recordings. This was also the case with the percentages ($M = 5.67\%$; SD = 4.68) beginning with remarks about properties and names of objects ($t = 0.03$; df = 23; Not significant). However, the percentages of mother-initiated exchanges beginning with remarks about names of objects, which had been very high in the first recording, decreased significantly ($t = 3.45$; df = 23; $p < 0.01$) during the second recording ($M = 56.39\%$; SD = 18.85). The percentages of mother-initiated exchanges beginning with remarks about locations of objects, as in (4.1), had been extremely low in the first recording ($M = 2.83\%$; SD = 6.24):

(4.1)   [Wayne (23:26) puts doll in cradle]
      Mother: Oh, in the bath.
      Wayne: Mmmm. Mmmm.

By the second recording, they had increased significantly ($t = 2.26$; df = 23; $p < 0.05$) to a somewhat higher level ($M = 6.44\%$ SD = 5.44). The same was true of the percentages of mother-initiated exchanges beginning with remarks about actions of objects, as in (4.2), which were extremely rare in the first recording ($M = 0.10\%$; SD = 0.51):

(4.2)   [Nicola (23:9) colours pictures]
      Mother: What are they doing?
      Nicola: Swimming.

By the second recording, they were significantly ($t = 5.41$; df = 23; $p < 0.001$) more frequent ($M = 8.52\%$; SD = 7.75). Finally, mother-initiated exchanges beginning with remarks about actions and names of objects, as in (4.3), had been virtually unknown in the first recording ($M = 0.96\%$; SD = 1.61):

(4.3)   [Jason (23:11) picks up jigsaw]
      Mother: And inside there are people buying things.
      Jason: Boy buy there.

By the second recording, they occurred significantly ($t = 5.05$; df = 23; $p < 0.001$) more often ($M = 6.00\%$; SD = 4.81).

(a) Request or provision of information

After looking at changes in the kind of information introduced, it is time to look at changes in the manner by which this information was introduced. The original expectation had been a general decrease in introduction via request rather than provision. However, the appearance of a group who produced extremely low percentages of mother-initiated exchanges beginning with requests for information during the first recording made an overall decrease seem much less likely. To find out exactly what did happen, the percentages of mother-initiated exchanges beginning with requests and provisions of information were computed for the second recording. These percentages are presented in Table 4.1. The mean and standard deviation of the percentages beginning with requests for information were computed for the excursive, recursive and discursive groups. The excursive group was, of course, the group who produced low percentages of these exchanges in the first recording, whereas the recursive and discursive groups were the groups who produced reasonably high percentages. The means and standard deviations are shown with the means and standard deviations for the first recording in Fig. 4.1.

Table 4.1. *Percentage of mother-initiated exchanges beginning with requests and provisions of information*

Name (group in brackets)	Requests information	Provides information	Total
Alan (E)	0 (0%)	3 (100.00%)	3
Barry (D)	5 (29.41%)	12 (70.59%)	17
Caroline (E)	11 (28.21%)	28 (71.79%)	39
Daniel (D)	14 (53.85%)	12 (46.15%)	26
Eileen (R)	19 (45.24%)	23 (54.76%)	42
Faye (R)	10 (66.67%)	5 (33.33%)	15
Graham (D)	53 (58.24%)	38 (41.76%)	91
Hayley (R)	14 (43.75%)	18 (56.25%)	32
Ian (R)	27 (50.00%)	27 (50.00%)	54
Jason (R)	12 (33.33%)	24 (66.67%)	36
Kevin (D)	24 (40.00%)	36 (60.00%)	60
Lucy (R)	12 (24.49%)	37 (75.51%)	49
Melanie (R)	3 (30.00%)	7 (70.00%)	10
Nicola (D)	48 (39.02%)	75 (60.98%)	123
Oliver (E)	20 (26.26%)	66 (76.74%)	86
Philip (R)	25 (65.79%)	13 (34.21%)	38
Richard (E)	22 (35.48%)	40 (64.52%)	62
Sally (D)	24 (39.34%)	37 (60.66%)	61
Tom (D)	7 (35.00%)	13 (65.00%)	20
Ursula (D)	11 (50.00%)	11 (50.00%)	22
Virginia (D)	39 (38.24%)	63 (61.76%)	102
Wayne (E)	26 (40.00%)	39 (60.00%)	65
Yvonne (D)	16 (30.77%)	36 (69.23%)	52
Zoe (D)	14 (31.11%)	31 (68.89%)	45

Figure 4.1 shows that the mean percentage of mother-initiated exchanges beginning with requests for information produced by the excursive group was much higher in the second recording. However, analysis by matched pairs t-test showed that the increase was not significant ($t = 1.47$; df $= 4$; Not significant). The insignificant increase could have been due to small changes in either the relative percentages of requests and provisions of information

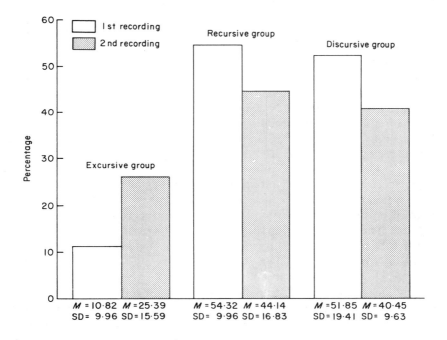

Figure 4.1: *Changes in the percentage of mother-initiated exchanges beginning with requests for information*

in the mothers' speech, or the relative percentages of requests and provisions of information receiving replies from the children. In fact, it was probably caused by the first factor. Further analysis showed that the percentages of requests for information in the mother's speech did increase somewhat at the expense of provisions ($t = 1.15$; df $= 4$; Not significant) from the first recording ($M = 20.93\%$; SD $= 11.81$) to the second ($M = 26.54\%$; SD $= 10.82$). Although the percentage of requests receiving replies also increased ($t = 1.75$; df $= 4$; Not significant) from the first recording ($M = 8.02\%$; SD $= 8.43$) to the second ($M = 28.13\%$; SD $= 17.56$), the percentage of provisions receiving replies showed a corresponding increase

($t = 2.19$; df $= 4$; Not significant) from the first recording ($M = 23.84\%$; SD $= 10.63$) to the second ($M = 36.73\%$; SD $= 10.97$). Hence, the increase was unlikely to reflect changes in the children's propensity to reply to requests for information in relation to their propensity to reply to provisions.

Figure 4.1 also shows that the mean percentages of mother-initiated exchanges beginning with requests for information produced by the recursive and discursive groups were much lower in the second recording. Again however, analysis by matched-pairs t-test showed that neither the decrease in the recursive group ($t = 1.94$; df $= 7$; Not significant) nor the decrease in the discursive group ($t = 2.11$; df $= 10$; Not significant) quite attained statistical significance. These marginal decreases can probably be partly attributed to changes in the relative percentages of requests and provisions of information in the mothers' speech. The recursive group showed a slight decrease ($t = 0.67$; df $= 7$; Not significant) in the percentage of requests in the mothers' speech from the first recording ($M = 30.83\%$; SD $= 10.13$) to the second ($M = 27.67\%$; SD $= 12.38$). The discursive group showed a similar decrease ($t = 1.10$; df $= 10$; Not significant) from the first recording ($M = 31.43\%$; SD $= 9.45$) to the second ($M = 28.02\%$; SD $= 6.55$). The slight decreases in mother-initiated exchanges beginning with requests for information can also be partly attributed to changes in the relative percentages of requests and provisions of information receiving replies from the children. The recursive group showed virtually no change ($t = 0.10$; df $= 7$; Not significant) in the percentage of requests receiving replies from the first recording ($M = 40.27\%$; SD $= 30.46$) to the second ($M = 39.15\%$; SD $= 8.19$). It showed a tiny increase ($t = 0.58$; df $= 7$; Not significant) in the percentage of provisions receiving replies from the first recording ($M = 14.87\%$; SD $= 17.51$) to the second ($M = 19.04\%$; SD $= 10.06$). The discursive group showed a sizeable increase in the percentage of requests receiving replies ($t = 1.96$; df $= 10$; Not significant) from the first recording ($M = 28.52\%$; SD $= 12.51$) to the second ($M = 41.26\%$; SD $= 18.64$). It showed an even greater increase in the percentage of provisions receiving replies ($t = 3.41$; df $= 10$; $p < 0.01$) from the first recording ($M = 11.84\%$; SD $= 5.13$) to the second ($M = 23.72\%$; SD $= 9.50$). Thus, the percentages of provisions receiving replies increased relatively more than the percentages of requests in both groups, although the absolute increase was more dramatic in the discursive group.

The increase in the percentage of mother-initiated exchanges beginning with requests for information produced by the excursive group and the decrease in the percentage of these exchanges produced by the recursive and discursive groups meant that the differences between the groups were smaller by the second recording. However, the mean difference between the excursive and discursive groups still reached statistical significance ($t = 2.34$; df $= 14$; $p < 0.05$), and the mean difference between the excursive and recursive groups fell only slightly below statistical significance ($t = 2.00$; df $= 11$; Not significant). Moreover, the mean difference between the recursive and discursive groups remained very small ($t = 0.60$; df $= 17$; Not significant). In the first recording, the group differences had been partly caused by mean differences in the percentages of requests for information in the mothers' speech. This was no longer the case by the second recording. In the second recording, neither the mean difference in the percentage of requests for information between the excursive and recursive groups ($t = 0.17$; df $= 11$; Not significant), nor the mean difference between the excursive and discursive groups ($t = 0.34$; df $= 14$; Not significant), nor the mean difference between the recursive and discursive groups ($t = 0.08$; df $= 17$; Not significant) even approached statistical significance. Rather, the group differences were due firstly to the children in the excursive group replying to somewhat fewer requests for information than the children in the recursive ($t = 1.55$; df $= 11$; Not significant) and discursive ($t = 1.33$; df $= 14$; Not significant) groups. The children in the recursive and discursive groups barely differed from each other ($t = 0.30$; df $= 17$; Not significant). The group differences were due secondly to the children in the excursive group replying to considerably more provisions of information than the children in the recursive ($t = 2.98$; df $= 11$; $p < 0.02$) and discursive groups ($t = 2.43$; df $= 14$; $p < 0.05$). Again, the children in the recursive and discursive groups barely differed from each other ($t = 1.03$; df $= 17$; Not significant).

(b) Minimal or extended replies

Having found rather complex changes in the percentages of mother-initiated exchanges beginning with requests for information, the analysis shifted to the percentages of mother-initiated exchanges ending with extended replies. As a preliminary, the children's replies were classified as minimal or extended. As in the first recording, most of their minimal replies were evaluative ($M = 85.72\%$; SD $= 17.78$), as in (4.4), rather than corrective, as in (4.5):

(4.4) [Yvonne (25:4) picks doll's brush up]
     Mother: That's a nice one, isn't it?
     Yvonne: No.

(4.5) [Richard (25:9) touches toes]
     Mother: Piggies.
     Richard: No, toes.
     Mother: Not piggies. Toes.

Most of their evaluative replies used imitation ($M = 74.44\%$; SD = 18.94), as in (4.6), rather than some non-imitative form, as in (4.7):

(4.6)   [Eileen (25:18) puts doll's bonnet on head]
        Mother: No, it's baby's hat.
        Eileen: Baby hat.

(4.7)   [Graham (23:5) looks at pictures]
        Mother: That's a bear on a scooter.
        Graham: Oh yes.

However, analysis by matched-pairs *t*-tests showed that imitative replies were significantly less frequent by the second recording ($t = 3.20$; df = 23; $p < 0.01$), although there was no significant change in the frequency of evaluative replies in general ($t = 1.10$; df = 23; Not significant). Chapter 1 cited studies by Moerk (1974, 1975), Nelson (1973a) and Seitz and Stewart (1975) that demonstrated an inverse relation between age and the incidence of imitation. The present results suggest that this could result from imitation being increasingly replaced by other evaluative expressions.

Having looked exclusively at minimal replies, the next step was to compare them with extended replies to see whether the tentatively hypothesized increase in the latter occurred in practice. The percentages of both minimal and extended replies are listed in Table 4.2. From figures in Table 4.2, the mean and standard deviation percentages of extended replies were computed for the three groups. These means and standard deviations are shown with the means and standard deviations from the first recording in Fig. 4.2. Rather surprisingly, the excursive group showed a slight decrease, which proved not to be significant on a matched-pairs *t*-test ($t = 0.26$; df = 4; Not significant). The discursive group showed a slight increase, which also proved not to be significant on a matched-pair *t*-test ($t = 0.45$; df = 10; Not significant). The only group to show any noticeable change was the recursive group. The mean percentage of mother-initiated exchanges ending with extended replies produced by the recursive group was significantly higher in the second recording than in the first ($t = 4.61$; df = 7; $p < 0.01$).

The mean percentage for the recursive group had, of course, been significantly lower than the mean percentages for the excursive and discursive groups during the first recording. Hence, it seemed likely that the changes over time had eradicated any differences between the groups. Analysis by *t*-test proved this to be the case. Neither the mean difference between the excursive and recursive groups ($t = 0.25$; df = 11; Not significant) nor the mean difference between the excursive and discursive groups ($t = 1.49$; df = 14; Not significant) nor the mean difference between the recursive and discursive groups ($t = 1.42$; df = 17; Not significant) turned out to be statistically significant.

Table 4.2. *Percentage of mother-initiated exchanges ending with minimal and extended replies*

Name (group in brackets)	Minimal reply	Extended reply	Total
Alan (E)	3 (100.00%)	0 (0%)	3
Barry (D)	14 (82.35%)	3 (17.65%)	17
Caroline (E)	35 (89.74%)	4 (10.26%)	39
Daniel (D)	23 (88.46%)	3 (11.54%)	26
Eileen (R)	39 (92.86%)	3 (7.14%)	42
Faye (R)	15 (100.00%)	0 (0%)	15
Graham (D)	86 (94.51%)	5 (5.49%)	91
Hayley (R)	26 (81.25%)	6 (18.75%)	32
Ian (R)	51 (94.44%)	3 (5.56%)	54
Jason (R)	34 (94.44%)	2 (5.56%)	36
Kevin (D)	44 (73.33%)	16 (26.67%)	60
Lucy (R)	47 (95.92%)	2 (4.08%)	49
Melanie (R)	9 (90.00%)	1 (10.00%)	10
Nicola (D)	111 (90.24%)	12 (9.76%)	123
Oliver (E)	76 (88.37%)	10 (11.63%)	86
Philip (R)	31 (81.58%)	7 (18.42%)	38
Richard (E)	59 (95.16%)	3 (4.84%)	62
Sally (D)	58 (95.08%)	3 (4.92%)	61
Tom (D)	15 (75.00%)	5 (25.00%)	20
Ursula (D)	18 (81.82%)	4 (18.18%)	22
Virginia (D)	92 (90.20%)	10 (9.80%)	102
Wayne (E)	57 (87.69%)	8 (12.31%)	65
Yvonne (D)	44 (84.62%)	8 (15.38%)	52
Zoe (D)	43 (95.56%)	2 (4.44%)	45

B. The changes in child-initiated exchanges

Moving onto conversational exchanges beginning with remarks from the children, it soon became apparent that they too had increased in frequency by the second recording. These 'child-initiated' exchanges occurred between 18 and 136 times ($M = 62.67$; SD $= 32.20$), an increase that was significant on a matched-pairs t-test ($t = 4.34$; df $= 23$; $p < 0.001$). The increase was partly due to the children addressing their mothers with significantly more ($t = 2.20$; df $= 23$; $p < 0.05$) remarks that requested or provided information ($M = 191.42$; SD $= 75.28$). However, it was also due to the mothers replying to significantly more ($t = 2.50$; df $= 23$; $p = 0.02$) of these remarks in the second recording ($M = 33.46\%$; SD $= 14.35$). Because child-initiated exchanges had increased in frequency, they were still more numerous than mother-initiated exchanges ($t = 5.50$; df $= 23$; $p < 0.001$). Moreover, they showed a similar tendency to become more diversified in informational content. Like mother-initiated exchanges, child-initiated exchanges were less likely ($t = 4.74$; df $= 23$; $p < 0.001$) to begin with remarks about names of objects in the second recording ($M = 63.39\%$; SD $= 18.88$), and similar likely ($t = 1.30$; df $= 23$; Not significant) to begin with remarks about properties of objects ($M = 5.08\%$; SD $= 8.29$). They were more likely ($t = 4.59$; df $= 23$; $p < 0.001$) to begin with remarks about actions of objects in the second recording ($M = 7.27\%$; SD $= 6.87$) than in the first ($M = 0.53\%$; SD $= 1.74$). Similarly, they were more likely ($t = 3.80$; df $= 23$; $p < 0.001$) to begin with remarks about actions and names of objects in the second recording ($M = 7.19\%$; SD $= 8.20$) than in the first ($M = 0.50\%$; SD $= 2.07$).

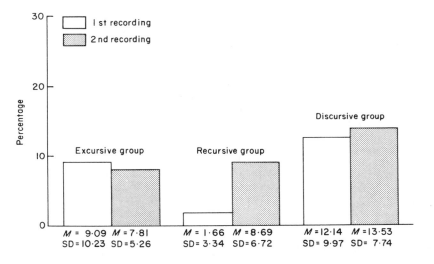

Figure 4.2: *Changes in the percentage of mother-initiated exchanges ending with extended replies*

(a) Request or provision of information

The central concern was however the percentages of child-initiated exchanges beginning with requests, rather than provisions of information. The relative percentages are presented in Table 4.3. From these figures, the mean and standard deviations of the percentages beginning with requests for information were computed for the excursive, recursive and discursive groups. As Fig. 4.3 shows, all three groups produced proportionately more

Table 4.3. *Percentage of child-initiated exchanges beginning with requests and provisions of information*

Name (group in brackets)	Requests information	Provides information	Total
Alan (E)	1 (4.55%)	21 (95.45%)	22
Barry (D)	4 (20.00%)	16 (80.00%)	20
Caroline (E)	10 (14.71%)	58 (85.29%)	68
Daniel (D)	18 (35.29%)	33 (64.71%)	51
Eileen (R)	5 (13.51%)	32 (86.49%)	37
Faye (R)	4 (19.05%)	17 (80.95%)	21
Graham (D)	8 (6.61%)	113 (93.39%)	121
Hayley (R)	4 (7.69%)	48 (92.31%)	52
Ian (R)	4 (5.13%)	74 (94.87%)	78
Jason (R)	1 (2.13%)	46 (97.87%)	47
Kevin (D)	1 (1.30%)	76 (98.70%)	77
Lucy (R)	2 (2.82%)	69 (97.18%)	71
Melanie (R)	4 (22.22%)	14 (77.78%)	18
Nicola (D)	2 (1.47%)	134 (98.53%)	136
Oliver (E)	1 (1.16%)	85 (98.84%)	86
Philip (R)	15 (27.27%)	40 (72.73%)	55
Richard (E)	4 (7.69%)	48 (92.31%)	52
Sally (D)	5 (5.15%)	92 (94.85%)	97
Tom (D)	0 (0%)	35 (100.00%)	35
Ursula (D)	0 (0%)	38 (100.00%)	38
Virginia (D)	0 (0%)	93 (100.00%)	93
Wayne (E)	0 (0%)	104 (100.00%)	104
Yvonne (D)	0 (0%)	74 (100.00%)	74
Zoe (D)	7 (13.73%)	44 (86.27%)	51

child-initiated exchanges beginning with requests in the second recording than in the first. This was, of course, what earlier research suggested. However, analysis by matched-pairs t-tests showed that neither the increase in the excursive group ($t = 1.21$; df = 4; Not significant), nor the increase in the recursive group ($t = 1.20$; df = 7; Not significant), nor the increase in the discursive group ($t = 0.89$; df = 10; Not significant) approached statistical significance. Even when the groups were combined, as seemed justified given no differences in the first recording, the mean percentage produced in the second recording ($M = 8.81\%$; SD = 9.83) was not significantly greater than the mean percentage produced in the first ($t = 1.80$; df = 23; Not significant).

The lack of marked increase in the percentages of child-initiated exchanges beginning with requests for information was almost certainly due to the lack of marked increase in the percentages of requests in the potentially conversational speech produced by the children. The percentages of requests ranged from 0 to 32.43 per cent ($M = 6.60\%$; SD = 7.44) in the second recording, which is not significantly different ($t = 1.38$; df = 23; Not significant) from the first recording. The results certainly did not reflect the percentages of requests receiving replies relative to the percentages of provisions. Both the percentages of requests receiving replies ($M = 43.32\%$; SD = 29.06) and the percentages of provisions ($M = 32.84\%$; SD = 14.54) were significantly higher in the second recording. However, the increase in the percentages of requests receiving replies ($t = 3.22$; df[1] = 17, $p < 0.01$) was larger than the increase in the percentages of provisions receiving replies ($t = 2.30$; df = 23; $p < 0.05$).

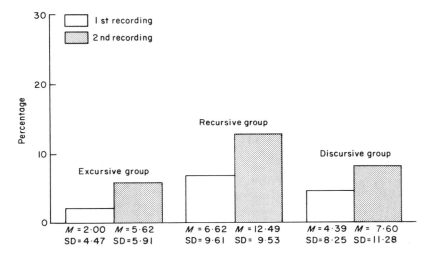

Figure 4.3: *Changes in the percentage of child-initiated exchanges beginning with requests for information*

(b) Minimal or extended replies

The results so far add up to a somewhat revised picture of changes over time in the pattern of mother – child conversation. Originally, the percentages of mother-initiated exchanges beginning with requests for information had been expected to decrease: they decreased insignificantly for the recursive and discursive groups and increased insignificantly for the excursive group. The percentages of mother-initiated exchanges ending with extended replies had been expected to increase: they increased significantly for the recursive group, but hardly changed for the excursive and discursive groups. The percentages of child-initiated exchanges beginning with requests for information had been expected to increase: they increased insignificantly for all three groups. The final expectation was an increase in child-initiated exchanges ending with extended replies, and this subsection will consider the issue, bearing in mind that the recursive group had more scope for increase than the excursive and discursive groups.

As a preliminary, the mothers' replies were classified as minimal or extended. Before comparing the percentages of minimal and extended replies, the minimal replies were considered separately, so that any changes in evaluative, as opposed to corrective, feedback and expansive, as opposed to other evaluative, feedback could be investigated. The percentages of remarks receiving evaluative feedback ($M = 82.82\%$; $SD = 9.34$), as in (4.8), rather than corrective feedback, as in (4.9), were virtually the same as in the first recording ($t = 0.27$; df $= 23$; Not significant):

(4.8)   [Melanie (23:15) gives hippo to mother]
    Melanie: Woof-woof.
    Mother: No, he don't go woof-woof.

(4.9)   [Kevin (23:27) looks at picture on block]
    Kevin: Tractor.
    Mother: Tractor?
                It's a little car.
    Kevin: Tractor.

Little change was also observed ($t = 0.85$; df $= 23$; Not significant) in the percentage of expansions ($M = 17.17\%$; $SD = 10.34$), such as mother's reply in (4.10), in total evaluative replies giving positive feedback:

(4.10)   [Eileen (25:18) picks doll up]
    Eileen: A shoes.
    Mother: Yes, she's got shoes on.

Next, the extended replies were also considered separately to investigate any changes in embedded extensions, as in (4.11), as opposed to separate extensions, as in (4.12):

(4.11)   [Nicola (23:9) draws picture]
    Nicola: Nose.
    Mother: He's got a pointed nose, hasn't he?

(4.12)   [Jason (23:11) looks at picture on block]
    Jason: Mouse.
    Mother: There's a beetle.
                He's got an umbrella.

The percentages of embedded extensions ($M = 55.94\%$; SD $= 21.35$) were not significantly higher than in the first recording ($t = 1.28$; df$^2 = 19$; Not significant).

The lack of change over time continued to be true for two of the groups when the percentages of extended, as opposed to minimal, replies were considered. The individual percentages are presented in Table 4.4. The means and standard deviations for the two recordings of the excursive, recursive and discursive groups are presented in Fig. 4.4. As Fig. 4.4 shows, the percentages produced by the excursive group were slightly lower in the second recording, although the difference was not significant on a matched-pairs t-test ($t = 0.35$; df $= 4$; Not significant). Similarly, the percentages produced by the discursive group were slightly higher in the second recording, but the difference was not significant on a matched-pairs t-test ($t = 0.33$;

Table 4.4. *Percentage of child-initiated exchanges ending with minimal and extended replies*

Name (group in brackets)	Minimal reply	Extended reply	Total
Alan (E)	18 (81.81%)	4 (18.18%)	22
Barry (D)	16 (80.00%)	4 (20.00%)	20
Caroline (E)	54 (79.41%)	14 (20.59%)	68
Daniel (D)	39 (76.47%)	12 (23.53%)	51
Eileen (R)	29 (78.38%)	8 (21.62%)	37
Faye (R)	17 (80.95%)	4 (19.05%)	21
Graham (D)	86 (71.07%)	35 (28.93%)	121
Hayley (R)	42 (80.77%)	10 (19.23%)	52
Ian (R)	57 (73.08%)	21 (26.92%)	78
Jason (R)	33 (70.21%)	14 (29.79%)	47
Kevin (D)	45 (58.44%)	32 (41.56%)	77
Lucy (R)	56 (78.87%)	15 (21.13%)	71
Melanie (R)	15 (83.33%)	3 (16.67%)	18
Nicola (D)	103 (75.74%)	33 (24.26%)	136
Oliver (E)	44 (51.16%)	42 (48.84%)	86
Philip (R)	47 (85.45%)	8 (14.55%)	55
Richard (E)	36 (69.23%)	16 (30.77%)	52
Sally (D)	70 (72.16%)	27 (27.84%)	97
Tom (D)	22 (62.86%)	13 (37.14%)	35
Ursula (D)	29 (76.32%)	9 (23.68%)	38
Virginia (D)	72 (77.42%)	21 (22.58%)	93
Wayne (E)	63 (60.58%)	41 (39.42%)	104
Yvonne (D)	45 (60.81%)	29 (39.19%)	74
Zoe (D)	41 (80.39%)	10 (19.61%)	51

df = 10; Not significant). It was only the percentages produced by the recursive group that were markedly higher in the second recording. Analysis by matched pairs *t*-test revealed that the increase was highly significant (*t* = 10.60; df = 7; *p* < 0.001).

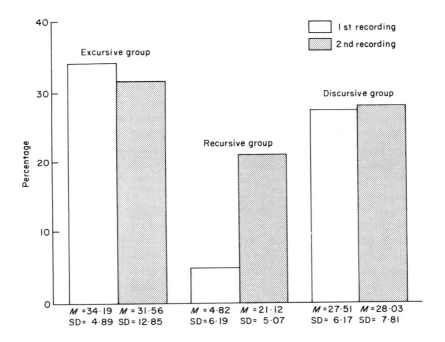

Figure 4.4: *Changes in the percentage of child-initiated exchanges ending with extended replies*

Despite its significance, the increase for the recursive group certainly did not eradicate the difference between the groups. In the recording, the mean difference between the recursive and excursive groups was almost significant (*t* = 2.09; df = 11; Not significant), and the mean difference between the recursive and discursive groups was significant (*t* = 2.18; df = 17; *p* < 0.05). Moreover, the mean difference between the excursive and discursive groups was far below statistical significance (*t* = 0.69; df = 14; Not significant).

C. The overall changes in mother – child conversation

Overall then, the present changes in mother – child conversation were somewhat different from the changes suggested by the psycholinguistic literature. The literature had suggested decreases in the percentages of mother-initiated exchanges beginning with requests rather than provisions of information: statistically insignificant decreases were observed in the recursive and discursive groups, but statistically insignificant increases were observed in the excursive group. It had suggested increases in the percentages of mother-initiated exchanges ending with extended, rather than minimal, replies: statistically significant increases were observed in the recursive group, but virtually no changes were observed in the excursive and discursive groups. The literature had suggested increases in the percentages of child-initiated exchanges beginning with requests rather than provisions of information: statistically insignificant increases were observed in all three groups. Finally, it had suggested increases in the percentages of child-initiated exchanges ending with extended, rather than minimal, replies: statistically significant increases were observed in the recursive group, but virtually no changes were observed in the excursive and discursive groups.

Reviewing these results suggests several points that might be emphasized. Firstly, the changes produced by the recursive group were always in the direction indicated by earlier work, although some of these changes were not statistically significant. The excursive and discursive groups sometimes produced no changes or even changes in the opposite direction. This was rather interesting, since the recursive group had conformed most closely to expectation in the first recording. Secondly, the statistical insignificance of most results meant that the global pattern of mother – child conversation had barely changed from the first recording to the second. In absolute terms, the percentages of mother-initiated exchanges beginning with requests rather than provisions of information were still rather low in the excursive group and reasonably high in the recursive and discursive groups. The percentages of mother-initiated exchanges ending with extended, rather than minimal, replies continued to be extremely low for all three groups. The same was true for the percentages of child-initiated exchanges beginning with requests rather than provisions of information. Finally, the percentages of child-initiated exchanges ending with extended, rather than minimal, replies remained fairly low for the recursive group and quite moderate for the excursive and discursive groups. The third and final point is a direct corollary of the second. The small changes in a context of global stability meant that most of the group differences were sustained, but slightly reduced in the second recording. The excursive group still produced considerably fewer mother-initiated exchanges beginning with requests for information than the recursive and discursive groups. The recursive group still produced considerably fewer child-initiated exchanges ending with extended replies than the excursive and discursive groups. Hence, mother – child conversation in the second recording was still characterized by three distinct patterns that were not dissimilar from the first recording. To underline this point, the chapter will conclude with lengthy extracts from second recording conversations held by the mothers and children who ended the previous chapter. The similarities between these extracts and their equivalents at the end of the previous chapter will be far more obvious than the differences. Thus when the next chapter discusses the wider implications of the results, it will be faced with a picture of considerable within-recording variation in mother – child conversation and little across-recording variation.

D. Extract from the second recording of an excursive mother – child pair

[Wayne (23:26) picks model lorry driver up]

Mother: A man.
Wayne: Eh man. Eh back.
Mother: Dustbin on his back.
            Dustbin on his back.
Wayne: On the back.
Mother: On the back.
Wayne: Eh door.
Mother: They come to the door, the door.
Wayne: Door.
Mother: There's the door.
Wayne: There door.
Mother: Uhm, you like Friday mornings, don't you?
            And then what do they do?
            Where do they put all the rubbish?
Wayne: Eh lorry.
Mother: In the lorry.

[Wayne looks at toy lorry]

Wayne: Lorry.
            No, down. Down.
Mother: Down. Down the hill.
            Oh, down the hill.
Wayne: Down.
Mother: Down.
            Fall down.
Wayne: Oh down.

E. Extract from the second recording of a recursive mother – child pair

[Mother shows picture to Ian (23:24)]
Mother: What's he doing?
Ian: This.
    Uhm, doing.
    That. Teeth.
Mother: Teeth, yes.
    Well what's that?
Ian: Mmmmmm. Don't know, Mum.
Mother: Oh, you do know.
    That's the toothpaste.
    He's cleaning his teeth, isn't he?
Ian: Yes.
[Mother turns page of book]
Mother: Now, what's he doing?
    What's that?
Ian: Chair.
Mother: Yes, there's a chair.
    Now, what's he got there?
Ian: Brush.
Mother: It's the bread, I think.
Ian: Bread.
Mother: Yes. Now what's he doing?
Ian: Walking.
Mother: Yes, he's walking.
Ian: Going somewhere.
Mother: Yes, he's going somewhere.

F. Extract from the second recording of a discursive mother – child pair

[Kevin (23:27) looks into box of model animals]
Mother: What's that monkey doing?
Kevin: Eating something.
    Tiger. Duck, look.
[Kevin picks penguin up]
Mother: What's that?
Kevin: Duck.
Mother: It's a penguin.
Kevin: Tiger.
    Eat it.
[Kevin eats penguin]
Mother: No. We don't eat penguins, do we?
Kevin: Penguin. Swimming.
[Kevin makes penguin swim]

Mother:	Yes, they do swim, don't they?
	They swim in cold water.
Kevin:	Cold water.
Mother:	Uhm, they like cold water, don't they?

[Kevin picks horse up]

Mother:	What's that?
Kevin:	Horse.
Mother:	Yes, what's he doing?
Kevin:	He kiss.
Mother:	What's he kissing?

[Kevin puts horse on penguin]

Kevin:	Baby. Kiss.

Notes

[1]The computation was based on 18 mother – child pairs because six children failed to request information in one of the two recordings.

[2]The computation was based on 20 mother – child pairs because four mothers gave no extended replies in the first recording.

5 Developmental Implications of the Conversational Exchanges

The data presented in Chapters 3 and 4 permit a tentative answer to the question that originally motivated the study. The question concerned the nature of mother – child conversation, and the tentative answer is that mother – child conversation can have one of three distinct patterns. It can have the pattern manifested by the excursive group, where mother-initiated exchanges virtually always began with the mothers providing information and ended with the children giving minimal replies. Child-initiated exchanges virtually always began with the children providing information, but ended with the mothers giving both minimal and extended replies. Alternatively, mother – child conversation can have the pattern manifested by the recursive group. Here, about half the mother-initiated exchanges began with the mothers providing information, and the other half began with the mothers requesting information. These exchanges nearly always ended with the children giving minimal replies. Child-initiated exchanges nearly always began with the children providing information and ended with the mothers giving minimal replies. Finally, mother – child conversation can have the pattern manifested by the discursive group. Here again, mother-initiated exchanges began with the mothers providing and requesting information in roughly equal proportions, but almost invariably ended with the children giving minimal replies. Child-initiated exchanges usually began with the children providing information, but ended with the mothers giving both minimal and extended replies.

Another way of expressing these conclusions is to say that up to four types of exchange appear with some frequency in mother – child conversations:

1. Mother-initiated exchanges beginning with requests for information and ending with minimal replies.
2. Mother-initiated exchanges beginning with provisions of information and ending with minimal replies.

3. Child-initiated exchanges beginning with provisions of information and ending with minimal replies.
4. Child-initiated exchanges beginning with provisions of information and ending with extended replies.

However, mother-initiated exchanges beginning with provisions of information and child-initiated exchanges ending with minimal replies appear frequently in all mother – child conversations. Mother-initiated exchanges beginning with requests for information and child-initiated exchanges ending with extended replies are sometimes quite unusual. This picture of part-uniformity and part-variability is extremely important in connection with the issue that prompted the interest in mother – child conversation in the first place. That issue was raised on the very first pages of this book, and amounted to whether mother – child conversation assists child language development. It should now be clear that all children will be assisted if mother-initiated exchanges beginning with provisions of information and child-initiated exchanges ending with minimal replies are helpful. However, some children will be helped more than others if mother-initiated exchanges beginning with requests for information and child-initiated exchanges ending with extended replies turn out to be useful.

A. The impact of mother-initiated exchanges

Before considering whether mother – child conversation assists child language development, it would be as well to reflect on two general issues. The first is how to define language development. The second is how the linguistic environment in general might assist language development. With respect to the first issue, the psycholinguistic literature contains many definitions of language development. However, there are certain advantages in choosing a definition that closely approximates the term's everyday usage. In which case, language development should be defined as acquiring skill at using language to perform the various communicative functions required in social interaction. Implicit in this definition is an emphasis firstly on use rather than understanding, and secondly on social interchange rather than solitary reflection. This means that developing any language, except a sign language for deaf people, involves acquiring skill at speaking rather than, on the one hand, listening and, on the other hand, writing.

Given this definition, the second issue can be rephrased in terms of the way in which the linguistic environment could foster the use of language in social interaction. In general, it seems that the linguistic environment could do this if it fulfilled one or both of two conditions. Firstly, it could help if it informed children about how their skills might be improved. Secondly, it could help if it motivated children (in the sense of giving them some 'raison d'être') to improve skills that they knew to be inadequate. The potentially informative role of the linguistic environment has long been recognized. Indeed, the sizeable body of research reviewed by Snow (1977b) and mentioned on the first pages of this book is exclusively concerned with that issue. Focusing on mothers' speech in general rather than mother – child conversation in particular, this research has shown that young children move in an environment that seems especially informative. In comparison with their speech to adults and older children, mothers' speech to young children is slow, simple and repetitive. Thus, new features are introduced gradually and emphatically, giving children every opportunity to extract them.

By way of contrast however, the potentially motivational role of the linguistic environment has never been seriously considered. This is probably because some once widely held beliefs about why children acquire their native language would preclude a motivational role altogether. These beliefs amount to assuming that children acquire their native language for much the same reason that linguists acquire esoteric foreign languages. In other words, children hold certain preconceptions about the nature of languages in general. They realize that testing their ideas involves learning some natural language. Their native language happens to be particularly convenient! Clearly if this picture were correct, children would not have to be motivated by any external agency. Their knowledge of how hypotheses must be tested would be sufficient motivation. However, it now seems highly unlikely that the picture is correct. Rather, the picture is generally regarded as seriously overestimating the intellectual capacities of young children. Thanks to the work of Inhelder and Piaget (1958), it is now known that before primary school age, children are simply incapable of the dispassionate curiosity required to acquire knowledge for its own sake. Before adolescence, children cannot acquire knowledge by the hypothetico-deductive method demanded of an embryonic linguist. Hence, when pre-school chldren learn their native language, they are no longer thought to be exploring the general structure of language. Rather, they are generally thought to be acquiring a tool that they find useful for communication.

In theory, deciding that young children do not act like linguists should mean reconsidering the motivational role of the linguistic environment. In practice, this has not happened. This continued neglect may be regarded as unfortunate, and so this chapter will consider the role of mother – child conversation in assisting child language development from both an informative and a motivational perspective. The first section will focus on mother-initiated exchanges. By the end, the advantage of this two fold perspective should be more apparent. This is because there will be little evidence that mother-initiated exchanges could inform children about improvements in their use of language. However, there will be grounds for supposing that mother-initiated exchanges beginning with requests for information might motivate children to improve certain aspects of these skills.

(a) Informative perspective

From points made in the introduction, it will come as no surprise to hear that the informative role of mother-initiated exchanges has been extensively discussed. The outcome of this discussion is that mother-initiated exchanges could play an informative role which is unique to them only if they prompt children into producing replies that are more sophisticated than their spontaneous remarks. The rationale for this conclusion is clear and fairly convincing. If children produce more sophisticated replies, they should notice the mismatch between these replies and the remarks they can habitually make. They should modify their conceptualization of language to accommodate the deviant cases, and their speech should become correspondingly more advanced. If children do not produce more sophisticated replies, they may still learn something from their mothers' antecedent remarks, particularly if these remarks have the helpful characteristics mentioned earlier. However, this is no more than they could have learned by listening in silence.

On further reflection, mother-initiated exchanges could only prompt children into making replies that are relatively sophisticated attempts to provide information. This is because children virtually always provide information when they participate in mother-initiated exchanges. It will be remembered that the mother–child conversations contained up to two types of mother-initiated exchange: those beginning with requests for information and ending with minimal replies, as in (5.1), and those beginning with provisions of information and ending with minimal replies, as in (5.2):

(5.1)   [Melanie (23:15) takes plate from toy box]
      Mother: What do you have on there?
      Melanie: Dinner.

(5.2)   [Barry (21:8) constructs model fireman]
      Mother: And that's his hat.
      Barry: Not.
              Not.

In minimal reply to a request for information, children will usually provide the missing information, as in (5.3):

(5.3)   [Mother shows model animal to Yvonne (22:0)]
  Mother: What's this one, Yvonne?
              What's this little one?
  Yvonne: It's monkey.

The only exceptions will be when they admit that they just 'don't know'. In minimal reply to a provision of information, children will usually repeat old information in evaluation, as in (5.4), or provide new information in correction, as in (5.5):

(5.4)   [Alan (22:9) looks at book]
  Mother: There's some big fishes.
  Alan: Big fishy.

(5.5)   [Nicola (23:9) gives sweet wrapper to mother]
  Mother: You've eaten it.
  [Nicola looks at me and smirks]
  Nicola: Lady ate it.

The only exceptions will be the seemingly rare occasions when children use forms like 'Yes' and 'No' to evaluate.

Although mother-initiated exchanges could only prompt children into making relatively sophisticated attempts to provide information, they have every opportunity to do this. As most writers would agree, early attempts to provide information are extremely rudimentary. Brown (1973), Clark (1973), McNeill (1970), Menyuk (1969) and Nelson (1973a) have discussed the grammatical aspects of these attempts. Their work suggests that when children first use language to provide information at about 18 months, they rely on solitary nouns chosen from a small set as in (5.6):

(5.6)   [Melanie (20:6) looks at me]
  Melanie: Eyes. Eyes.
  Mother: Eyes?

The use of solitary nouns precludes expressions with subject pronouns, as in (5.7), not to mention well formed sentences, as in (5.8):

(5.7)   [Barry (21:8) fingers model animal]
  Barry: It tiger.
  Mother: That's a lion.

(5.8)   [Hayley (20:11) looks at doll]
  Hayley: It's a baby.
  Mother: Uhm.

The use of nouns chosen from a small set leads to 'overextension', where words are applied to manifestly inappropriate referents, as in (5.9):

(5.9)   [Jason (20:16) picks Dougall up]
   Jason: Teddy.
   Mother: It's not a teddy.

The semantic aspects of early attempts to provide information have been discussed by Bloom (1973), Greenfield and Smith (1976) and Rodgon (1976). Data presented by these writers imply that for 18-month-old children, providing information involves naming the objects they are currently manipulating or observing. It rarely involves mentioning other features of these objects, such as their quantities, properties, owners, locations and actions. Thus, remarks, like the child's contribution to (5.10), that mention a property seem to be very unusual:

(5.10) [Virginia (21:17) cuddles doll]
   Virginia: She cold, Mum.
   Mother: Cold.

The same seems to be true of remarks, like the child's contribution to (5.11), that name the object of current interest and then mention another feature:

(5.11) [Oliver (23:19) tips doll out of cradle]
   Oliver: Oh Olliga fall down.
                Olliga fall down there.
   Mother: Oh poor Olliga.

Thus, mothers have every opportunity to coax children into giving replies that are more sophisticated than their spontaneous attempts to provide information. The question is whether they do so. In answer to this question, most psycholinguists have assumed that children's replies are no more sophisticated than their spontaneous remarks in a semantic sense. Interestingly, data presented in Chapters 3 and 4 can be used to support this assumption. To give semantically sophisticated replies, children would have to mention features other than names of currently focal objects, either singly or in combination. Mentioning such features in reply to remarks about names, as in (5.12), would constitute 'extended replies':

(5.12) [Mother and Sally (23:8) look at pictures]
   Mother: Who's this?
   Sally: Boy.
                Boy down floor.

Chapters 3 and 4 pointed out that most mother-initiated exchanges began with remarks about names of objects in both the first and the second recordings. Given that mother-initiated exchanges rarely ended with extended replies in either recording, this means that the children must seldom have given semantically sophisticated replies.

In addition, most psycholinguists have assumed that children's replies to requests for information are no more sophisticated than their spontaneous remarks in a grammatical sense. This assumption seems quite reasonable, since requests for information are grammatically quite unlike their legitimate replies. However, psycholinguists have gradually changed their views about the grammatical sophistication of children's replies to provisions of information. As Chapters 3 and 4 have underlined, such replies are predominantly imitative, as in (5.13):

(5.13) [Oliver (20:10) watches as mother picks model chimpanzee up]
    Mother: Look, a little monkey.
    Oliver: Monkey.

Until the 1960s, it was widely assumed that imitations were grammatically more sophisticated than spontaneous remarks, in the sense of being better formed. This assumption seemed in need of reappraisal when Brown and Fraser (1963) and Ervin (1964) presented data indicating that imitative speech is no better formed than spontaneous speech. In fact, Brown and Fraser demonstrated that precisely the same types of words are omitted from both kinds of speech. In their study, 2- to 3-year-old children omitted articles, auxiliaries, copulas and inflections and included adjectives, nouns and verbs when asked to 'Say what I say' and when talking non-imitatively. Possible counter-evidence appeared in Fraser *et al.*'s (1963) study with 3- to 4-year olds, and its replication by Lovell and Dixon (1965) with 2- to 6-year-olds. In these studies, children were asked to imitate pairs of sentences such as 'The sheep is walking' and 'The sheep are walking'. Then, they were asked to listen to these sentences and produce them when the experimenter pointed to appropriate pictures. Children generally gave better formed responses on the former 'imitation' task than on the latter 'production' task. Although this finding has been widely interpreted as demonstrating that imitative speech is better formed than spontaneous speech, it should actually be treated with caution. Because the experimenter read the sentences before the production task, the children may have felt they were expected to reproduce the experimenter's exact words. In that case, the finding would amount to a comparison between an easy imitation task and a more difficult imitation task.

Grammatical development is not simply a question of better formed expressions. It is also a question of wider vocabulary, and quite recent research suggested that children might introduce new words imitatively. For instance, Bloom *et al.* (1974) and Ryan (1973) reported that the words young children imitated were quite different from the words they used spontaneously. Moreover, words were often used imitatively before they were used spontaneously, suggesting that they might have been introduced via imitation. Unfortunately as Leonard and Kaplan (1976) have pointed out, this shift from imitative to spontaneous use does not prove that words are consistently introduced imitatively. Leonard and Kaplan described a study in which they taught four new words to young children and recorded the context in which these words were first used. Well over half the initial usage was spontaneous rather than imitative. In the light of this finding, there are really no grounds for supposing imitation plays a special part in the introduction of new words.

Thus, research on imitation is leading to one disappointing conclusion about the informative role of mother-initiated exchanges. It was suggested that mother-initiated exchanges could only play this role if they caused children to produce replies that were more sophisticated than their spontaneous speech. It was then argued that mother-initiated exchanges had every opportunity to elicit provisions of information that were relatively sophisticated, in both a semantic and a grammatical sense. However, it has always been assumed that children's replies are semantically no more sophisticated. It has also been assumed that children's replies to requests for information are grammatically no more sophisticated. Both assumptions seem *prima facie* reasonable. It no longer looks as if imitative replies to provisions of information are grammatically advanced. Faced with current data demonstrating that children's replies to provisions of information are predominantly imitative, it must now seem unlikely that mother-initiated exchanges play any role in informing children about potential improvements in their use of language.

(b) Motivational perspective

However, this does not necessarily mean that mother-initiated exchanges play no role at all in fostering linguistic skills. In the introduction to this section, it was suggested that mother-initiated exchanges need not only play an informative role. They might also motivate children to improve skills that are known to be inadequate. Hence, this subsection will consider whether mother-initiated exchanges could elicit reactions from children that might motivate them to improve their skill at using language.

One reaction that mother-initiated exchanges will certainly evoke in their child participants is an expectation about conversational role. Mother-initiated exchanges beginning with requests for information, such as those in (5.14), will lead children to expect the role of providing new information:

(5.14) [Mother sits Philip (24:5) on her lap]
        Mother: What can you see?
                    What's this?
        Philip: Doggie.
        Mother: And what's this?
        Philip: Doggie.
        Mother: What's that?
        Philip: Pussy cat.
                    Baba.

Mother-initiated exchanges beginning with provisions of information, such as those in (5.15), will lead children to expect the role of acknowledging information that has already been provided:

(5.15) [Oliver (20:10) takes zookeeper from mother]
        Mother: That's a man, isn't it?
        Oliver: Man.
        Mother: That's his brush.
        Oliver: Brush.
        Mother: It has to go back in his hands.
                    Like that. Into his little hand.
        Oliver: In.

Now performing the role of providing new information in response to requests involves spontaneously producing some particular information. Hence, it would be impossible to perform this role without pre-existing knowledge of the particular information that might be requested and the particular expressions that might provide it. However, performing the role of acknowledging information that has already been provided does not involve spontaneously producing some particular information. Hence, it would be quite easy to perform this role without pre-existing knowledge of the information that might be requested, or the expressions that might be used to provide it. This role could be adequately performed by learning firstly to recognize when information in general has been provided and secondly to mutter 'Uh-hu', 'Yes' or some partial imitation in response.

Thus, children who adopt the role of providing requested information should have more incentive to develop certain aspects of providing information than children who adopt the role of acknowledging provided information. In particular, they should feel more motivated to learn precisely what kinds of information can be provided and in what combinations. They should feel more motivated to learn the vocabulary for providing information including a wider range of nouns for naming objects. Their greater motivation to adopt well formed expressions is more questionable. Complete sentences are not obligatory in reply to requests for information; predicate phrases will suffice, as (5.16) and (5.17) illustrate:

(5.16) [Eileen (25:18) and mother play with model animals]
    Mother: What's that?
    Eileen: A horsie.

(5.17) [Barry (24:27) picks block up]
    Mother: What are you doing?
    Barry: Putting it away.

Overall though, it could be argued that mother-initiated exchanges beginning with requests for information seem to place conversational demands on children that might motivate them to develop many aspects of using language to provide information. Participation in mother-initiated exchanges beginning with provisions of information seems to place conversational demands on children that should have little motivational impact.

Although these ideas may have some intuitive plausibility, they are not at present supported by empirical research. However, they are not seriously challenged by available data. Perhaps the closest to counter-evidence appears in the study of Cross (1977, 1978), which was summarized in Chapter 1. As part of this study, Cross compared mothers' speech to children showing 'accelerated' language development with mothers' speech to children showing 'normal' language development. The finding which has some relevance for the present discussion and which has been confirmed to some extent by Wells (1979) was the absence of difference between the two groups of mothers on their percentages of *wh*-questions. However, there are at least three reasons for discounting the criticism implicit in this finding. Firstly, *wh*-questions can be used for purposes other than requesting information. Secondly, *wh*-questions do not necessarily initiate conversations, even when they are used as requests for information. Indeed, Chapters 3 and 4 showed that the incidence of mother-initiated exchanges beginning with requests for information was only partly influenced by the incidence of requests from the mothers. It was also influenced by the incidence of requests receiving replies from the children. Finally, Cross defined her 'accelerated' and 'normal' groups on measures relating to skill at using well formed sentences. The present ideas are explicitly restricted to other aspects of language development. In the light of this, there still seems a distinct possibility that mother-initiated exchanges beginning with requests for information might motivate children to develop the specified aspects of providing information.

Confirming this possibility would imply that children differ in the extent to which their language development is assisted by mother-initiated exchanges. Chapters 3 and 4 revealed considerable variation in the putatively helpful mother-initiated exchanges beginning with requests for information. The mothers and children in the excursive group rarely held these exchanges. However, they accounted for about half of the mother-initiated exchanges held by the mothers and children in the recursive and discursive groups. Thus, the present suggestion that mother-initiated exchanges beginning with requests for information are more helpful than mother-initiated exchanges beginning with provisions of information implies that children who hold conversations like the excursive group will receive less assistance than children who held conversations like the recursive and discursive groups.

B. The impact of child-initiated exchanges

Having reached this conclusion about mother-initiated exchanges, it is time to consider child-initiated exchanges. It will be remembered that mother – child conversation also contained up to two types of child-initiated exchange: those beginning with provisions of information and ending with minimal replies, as in (5.18), and those beginning with provisions of information and ending with extended replies, as in (5.19):

(5.18) [Lucy (20:7) feeds doll]
    Lucy: Baby drink.
             Drink.
             Drink.
    Mother: Drink, yes.

(5.19) [Jason (23:11) looks at blocks]
    Jason: Train. Train.
             Train.
    Mother: Train.
             And it's got a station there.
             With a signal.

This section will discuss the role of both types of child-initiated exchange in fostering skill at using language to perform various communicative functions. It will approach the issue from both an informative and a motivational perspective. Like the preceding section, it will discover that the informative value of child-initiated exchanges has been extensively discussed in the psycholinguistic literature. However, their motivational value has been virtually ignored. Although this one-sidedness is theoretically undesirable, this section will conclude that empirically it is less consequential. This is because it will propose that child-initiated exchanges are unlikely to play more than an informative role.

(a) Informative perspective

Reviewing the psycholinguistic literature reveals considerable tacit consensus over the circumstances in which child-initiated exchanges will inform children about potential improvements in using language. With rare exceptions, it implies that these exchanges must contain replies from mothers that are more sophisticated than their children's antecedent remarks. In these circumstances, children should compare their inadequate renderings with their mothers' superior efforts. Having noticed the inconsistencies, they will modify their own performance. Of course, child-initiated exchanges could only contain replies that are relatively sophisticated attempts to provide information. This follows from the point made in the previous paragraph, that child-initiated exchanges almost always began with provisions of information. Nevertheless, this still leaves plenty of scope for mothers to provide relatively sophisticated replies. As the previous section pointed out, children's skill at providing information has to develop grammatically and semantically. Grammatically, children must move from using solitary nouns chosen from a small set towards using well formed sentences with a wide range of nouns. Semantically, they must move from naming the objects they are observing or manipulating, towards mentioning features other than names, and combining several of these features in single remarks. This suggests that any maternal reply that is better formed than its antecedent or that provides an alternative name can be regarded as relatively sophisticated in a grammatical sense. Any maternal reply to an antecedent object name that mentions a feature other than the name either singly or in combination can be regarded as relatively sophisticated in a semantic sense.

If this fourfold definition of relative sophistication can be taken for granted, it will be immediately clear that mothers' replies are often more sophisticated than their antecedents. Looking first at exchanges in which mothers reply minimally to information provided by their children, enough has been said in previous chapters to show that these exchanges can end with remarks that are better formed than their antecedents. Specifically, the present study, together with the sizeable body of previous work summarized in Chapter 1, have shown that mothers sometimes make minimal replies by 'expanding' their children's incomplete remarks into well formed sentences, as in (5.20):

(5.20) [Lucy (20:7) throws dog's bowl]
     Lucy: Kim.
     Mother: Yes, it's Kim's.

On further reflection, exchanges in which mothers give minimal replies to information provided by their children can also supply alternative names for objects. In Chapters 3 and 4, it became clear that a large proportion of child-initiated exchanges begin with remarks about names of objects. As the mean percentages were 83 per cent in the first recording and 63 per cent in the second, it would be fair to say that remarks about names of objects predominated in child-initiated exchanges. Moreover, in both recordings, about one in six child-initiated exchanges ending with minimal replies involved corrective rather than evaluative feedback. Despite somewhat different computational methods, this compares well with the percentages of maternal corrections reported by Lieven (1978a) and Moerk (1974, 1975, 1976) in studies described in earlier chapters. Now if child-initiated exchanges often begin with object names and occasionally end with corrective replies, it follows that mothers must sometimes give replies, as in (5.21), that supply alternative names:

(5.21) [Alan (22:9) picks comic up]
    Alan: Pussy.
    Mother: Pussy cat, yes.
               It's Tom.

Extended replies were defined as replies that fulfilled the requirements for minimal replies, but also requested or provided new information about the same subject or old information about a new subject. Insofar as they incorporate minimal replies, they must also contain expansions that demonstrate better formed alternatives and corrections that provide alternative object names. However, they can also transcend their antecedents in semantic sophistication. When the children's antecedent remarks specify names of objects as they generally seem to do, extended replies, like the mother's response in (5.22), must almost by definition mention features other than object names:

(5.22) [Graham (23:5) looks at picture]
    Graham: Plane.
    Mother: Plane, yes.
               Here it is and it goes right through here.

When mothers' extended replies are embedded in their minimal concomitants, as in both (5.23) and about half of the extended replies considered in Chapters 3 and 4, they must necessarily demonstrate that several features can be incorporated in single remarks:

(5.23) [Ursula (24:22) gives animal to mother]
    Ursula: Walrus.
    Mother: Walrus has lost his tusks, hasn't he?

Thus, mothers do produce replies that are relatively sophisticated in both a grammatical and a semantic sense. In doing this, they produce replies that fulfil the presumed requirements for informing children about the grammatical and semantic development of skill at using language. Whether children actually use this information is a different question altogether, and is not easily answered on the basis of existing research. This is partly because research has concentrated on relations between maternal replies and the adoption of well formed expressions. It has more or less overlooked other aspects of language development. It is also because the results of the research are extremely confusing.

The pioneering study on relations between maternal expansion and well formed speech was conducted by Cazden (and reported in Brown *et al.*, 1969). Cazden interacted over a 3-month period with three groups of children aged 28–38 months at the start of her study. One group received expansions in reply to their speech; the second received well formed sentences that were not expansions and the third acted as a control and received no special treatment. The first group did not differ from the control on any of six measures of well formed speech. However by way of complete contrast, Nelson *et al.* (1973) exposed three groups of children, who were of similar age to Cazden's, to similar treatments over a similar time period using similar measures of development. They found that their expansion group was superior to the control group on virtually every measure. There have not been any satisfactory attempts to reconcile these studies, and the relation between expansion and the adoption of well formed expressions is usually treated as an open question.

Existing research is even less clear about the relation between mothers' corrections and the acquisition of more varied object names, mothers' extended replies and the discussion of features other than names, and mothers' embedded extensions and the incorporation of several features in single remarks. Virtually nothing is known about the impact of correction on any aspect of language development. Indeed, research in this area has more or less stopped at demonstrating, via examples like (5.24) and (5.25), that correction has little immediate impact, no doubt assuming that it cannot therefore have any long-term impact:

(5.24) [Sally (20:8) looks at picture in book]
   Mother: What's driving the water?
   Sally: Teatoc.
       Teatoc.
   Mother: Teapot, not a teatoc.
   Sally: Tea—
   Mother: —Pot.
   Sally: Tea—

Mother:	—Pot.
Sally:	Teatoc. Teatoc.

(5.25) [Sally (23:8) pours water into cup]

Sally:	A teatop. Teatop.
	Teatop. Teatop.
Mother:	It's a teapot.
Sally:	Teatop.
Mother:	Teapot, not a teatop.
	Teapot.
Sally:	Sugar.

Virtually all research into the impact of extended replies has been concerned with well formed sentences, and unfortunately the results of this research are less than straightforward. Although the impact of extended replies on the hitherto unconsidered semantic aspects of language development might seem more interesting, it is perfectly reasonable to expect a relation between extended replies and the use of well formed speech. Extended replies incorporate minimal replies, and minimal replies sometimes contain expansions. Consequently, it is not surprising to find that Cross' (1978) 'accelerated' group experienced proportionately more extended replies than her 'normal' group. Equally predictable is Wells' (1979) discovery of positive correlations between frequency of maternal extension and progress towards well formedness in his longitudinal study of 128 children. The problems arise with the experimental studies of Cazden (in Brown *et al.*, 1969) and Nelson *et al.* (1973). From the account of Brown *et al.* (1969), it is clear that dual pressures to sustain conversation and avoid expansion meant that the second group in these studies was exposed to extended replies without expansion. Not surprisingly, the second group in the study of Nelson *et al.* (1973) did not differ from the control group on any measure of well formedness. However, the second group in Brown *et al.*'s (1969) study showed faster development than both the control and the expansion groups!

(b) Motivational perspective

In the light of this research, the following conclusion should probably be drawn about the role of child-initiated exchanges in informing children about potential improvements in providing information. Child-initiated exchanges ending with minimal replies could inform children about improvements in the grammar of providing information. Child-initiated exchanges ending with extended replies could inform children about improvements in the grammar and semantics of providing information. However, omissions and contradictions in existing research preclude any final decision about whether these theoretically possible roles are performed in practice. Leaving the subject at this unsatisfactory stage, it is now time to discuss the motivational role of child-initiated exchanges. (5.26) and (5.27) are presented as a prelude to this discussion:

(5.26) [Ian (21:0) picks stacking ring up]
     Ian: Play that.
     Mother: You're going to play with that, eh?
     Ian: Mummy, you play that.

(5.27) [Yvonne (25:4) draws]
     Yvonne: Mummy hair.
     Mother: Shall Mummy do some hair?
     Yvonne: It's Mummy hair.

The children's second remarks in (5.26) and (5.27) suggest that their mothers had completely misunderstood the communicative function of their first remarks. In (5.26), an attempt to direct behaviour was seemingly misinterpreted as an attempt to provide information. In (5.27), an attempt to provide information was seemingly misinterpreted as an attempt to direct behaviour. It seems possible that such misinterpretations make children realize the inadequacies of their speech for performing the communicative function in question. In doing this, the misinterpretations may motivate them to adopt more advanced speech. If this seems plausible, it becomes expedient to ask whether maternal misinterpretations occur in conversational exchanges initiated by children. The answer is of course negative. Child-initiated exchanges were only regarded as conversational where there were grounds for believing that the mothers' responses were appropriate. Thus, the child-initiated exchanges under consideration could not fulfil the postulated conditions for motivating children to develop their skill at using language. As it is hard to imagine child-initiated exchanges motivating under other conditions, it begins to look as if the child-initiated exchanges under consideration do not play a motivating role.

This leaves them with the theoretically plausible, but empirically unsubstantiated, informative role summarized at the beginning of this subsection. If they have this role and no other, children must differ in the assistance they can derive from child-initiated exchanges. In particular, children who hold conversations like the recursive group should not be able to derive as much information as children who hold conversations like the excursive and discursive groups. This is because the child-initiated exchanges experienced by the children in the recursive group nearly always ended with minimal replies. The child-initiated exchanges experienced by the children in the excursive and discursive groups ended with minimal and extended replies. Both minimal and extended replies were believed to contain expansions and corrections that yield information about the grammatical aspects of providing information. Assuming the groups did not differ in their percentages of expansions and corrections in mothers' replies,[1] children should have equal access to grammatical information. However, only extended replies were believed to yield information relevant to the semantic aspects of providing information. Hence, the children in the recursive group should have less access to semantic information.

C. The overall impact of mother – child conversation

Given these conclusions about child-initiated exchanges, it is now possible to present an overall picture of how mother – child conversation might facilitate child language development. At the start of this chapter, language development was defined as the acquisition of skill in using language to perform various communicative functions. Taking this definition for granted, it was felt that the linguistic environment in general, and mother – child conversation in particular, might facilitate language development if they performed one or both of two roles. Firstly, they might facilitate language development if they informed children about potential improvements in their use of language. Secondly, they might facilitate language development if they motivated children to make these improvements. The remainder of this chapter considered whether these roles might be performed by exchanges that occurred frequently in mother – child conversation. It also considered the implications of differences in the occurrence of exchanges that were thought to assist language development.

Data presented in Chapters 3 and 4 indicated that two types of mother-initiated exchange could occur frequently in mother – child conversation. They were mother-initiated exchanges beginning with requests for information and ending with minimal replies, and mother-initiated exchanges beginning with provisions of information and ending with minimal replies. After lengthy theoretical and empirical discussion, it was felt that neither type of exchange could inform children about potential improvements in their use of language. However, mother-initiated exchanges beginning with requests for information might motivate children to improve certain aspects of using language to provide information. In particular, they might motivate children to use a wider range of nouns when naming the objects they were engaged with, to mention other features of the objects and to incorporate several features of the objects into single remarks.

Moving onto child-initiated exchanges, it was apparent that they also fell into two main types. These were child-initiated exchanges beginning with provisions of information and ending with minimal replies, and child-initiated exchanges beginning with provisions of information and ending with extended replies. In contrast to the mother-initiated exchanges, it was felt that neither type of child-initiated exchange was likely to play a motivational role. However, child-initiated exchanges ending with minimal replies had the potential to inform children about grammatical aspects of providing information. Particular mention was made of their potential for informing children about better formed expressions and new nouns for naming objects. Child-initiated exchanges ending with extended replies not only had the potential to yield grammatical information. They could also have informed about the semantic aspects of providing information, particularly the single or combined usage of features other than object names.

If these conclusions are correct, they imply marked differences in the assistance children can derive from conversation with their mothers. Children who participate in conversations like the excursive group rarely experience mother-initiated exchanges beginning with requests for information, but frequently experience child-initiated exchanges ending with extended replies. In comparison with other children, they should derive little assistance from mother-initiated exchanges, but maximal assistance from child-initiated exchanges. Children who participate in conversations like the recursive group frequently experience mother-initiated exchanges beginning with requests for information, but rarely experience child-initiated exchanges ending with extended replies. In comparison with other children, they should derive considerable assistance from mother-initiated exchanges, but limited assistance from child-initiated exchanges. Finally, children who participte in conversations like the discursive group frequently experience both mother-initiated exchanges beginning with requests for information and child-initiated exchanges ending with extended replies. In comparison with other children, they should derive considerable assistance from both mother- and child-initiated exchanges. Given these implications, it seems particularly important to see whether the theoretical conclusions are correct. Specifically, it seems important to see how more convincing empirical evidence could be produced. This will be the concern of the next chapter.

Notes

[1]They seemed not to differ. One-way analyses of variance revealed no group differences in the percentages of expansions in mothers' replies giving positive feedback during either the first ($F = 0.16$; df $= 2/21$; Not significant) or the second ($F = 1.59$; df $= 2/21$; Not significant) recordings. Likewise, they revealed no group differences in the percentages of corrections in mothers' total replies during either the first ($F = 1.03$; df $= 2/21$; Not significant) or the second ($F = 1.08$; df $= 2/21$; Not significant) recordings.

6 Empirical Evidence for the Developmental Implications

The previous chapter considered the developmental significance of the four types of exchange that occurred with some frequency in mother-child conversation. After much theoretical deliberation, it was concluded that mother-initiated exchanges beginning with requests for information might motivate children to improve certain aspects of providing information. These aspects related to the range of nouns used to name objects, the specification of features of objects other than their names (to be called 'non-names') and the incorporation of several features of objects into single remarks (to be called 'feature combinations'). Mother-initiated exchanges beginning with provisions of information should not motivate children to develop these or any other aspects of language. Because they contained expansions and corrections, child-initiated exchanges ending with minimal replies might inform children about better formed expressions for providing information and wider ranges of nouns for naming objects. Because they also contained expansions and corrections, child-initiated exchanges ending with extended replies could yield all the information provided by their counterparts ending with minimal replies. However, they might also inform children that non-names and feature combinations can be provided.

Given the conversational patterns described in Chapters 3 and 4 these conclusions imply differences in the assistance children can derive from conversations with their mothers. The conversational patterns produced by the mothers and children in the excursive group involved reasonably high frequencies of mother-initiated exchanges beginning with provisions of information, child-initiated exchanges ending with minimal replies, and child-initiated exchanges ending with extended replies. It involved extremely low frequencies of mother-initiated exchanges beginning with requests for information. If the model summarized in the previous paragraph is correct, children who participate in conversations like the excursive group receive relatively little incentive to develop their skill at providing object names, non-names and feature combinations. They are relatively well informed about these aspects of providing information and the use of well formed expressions. The conversational patterns produced by the mothers and children in the recursive group involved reasonably high frequencies of mother-initiated exchanges beginning with requests for information, mother-initiated exchanges beginning with provisions of information and child-initiated exchanges ending with minimal replies. It involved extremely low frequencies of child-initiated exchanges ending with extended replies. Here, the model implies that children who participate in conversations like the recursive group receive relatively high incentive to develop their skill at providing object names, non-names and feature combinations. However, they are only well informed about new object names and well formed expressions. Finally, the conversational patterns produced by the mothers and children in the discursive group involved reasonably high frequencies of all four types of exchange. Hence, children who participate in conversations like the discursive group not only receive plenty of incentive to develop in the areas of interest, but they should also find their mothers' replies relatively informative about new object names, well formed expressions, non-names and feature combinations.

Assuming children who participate in the different kinds of conversation are comparable in all respects except their conversational patterns, these suggestions imply group differences in developing skill at providing information. Firstly, they imply that children who participate in conversations like the excursive group should be slower than other children at broadening the range of object names they provide (E < R = D). Although receiving as much information about alternative object names, these children receive less incentive to use available information. Secondly, the suggestions imply that children who participate in conversations like the excursive and recursive groups should be slower than other children at providing non-names and feature combinations (E < D and R < D). Children who participate in conversations like the excursive group receive as much information about providing non-names and feature combinations as children who participate in conversations like the discursive group. However, they receive less incentive to use it. Children who participate in conversations like the recursive group receive as much incentive to mention non-names and feature combinations as children who participate in conversations like the discursive group. However, they receive less information about these aspects of providing information. No predictions can be made about the provision of non-names and feature combinations by children who participate in conversations like the excursive and recursive groups. This is because the relative contribution of low incentive and low information cannot be assessed. Although the suggestions predict group differences in incorporating new names, non-names and feature combinations, they do not predict group differences in adopting well formed expressions to provide information. There was no reason to suppose the children in the excursive group would feel less motivated in this area. There was every reason to suppose the children in the recursive group would feel as well informed.

Given children who were comparable in all respects except mother – child conversation, the model summarized earlier implies these group differences in skill at providing information. Hence, the presence of these group differences in such circumstances would constitute strong evidence for the model. Their absence would constitute strong evidence against the model. Of course, children are not only learning to provide information during the latter half of their second year. They are also learning to perform many other communicative functions, of which directing behaviour and requesting information are probably the most important. It is possible that any group differences in skill at providing information would be reflected in skill at performing other communicative functions. Although possible, this is by no means certain. Taking it for granted would entail making certain, potentially controversial assumptions. Hence, the presence or absence of group differences in performing other communicative functions would be somewhat ambiguous, even assuming otherwise comparable children. As the presence or absence of group differences in skill at providing information would not suffer from these ambiguities, it seems advisable to focus on this aspect of language development. In the light of this, the next problem is how to find out whether children who differ only in their conversational patterns do in fact produce the predicted differences in skill at providing information.

The issue could be researched most efficiently by randomly assigning mothers and children to three groups, persuading them to simulate the three conversational patterns while holding other aspects of their interaction constant, and comparing skill at providing information across groups. Unfortunately, the first section will show that this strategy is ethically and practically infeasible. The incidence of group differences between children who varied only in their conversational experiences could however be assessed by a second, less efficient strategy. This strategy involves two steps. The first would amount to finding groups of mothers and children who naturally employed the three conversational patterns and comparing skill at providing information across groups. If the predicted differences emerged, a second step must be taken. This would involve further research to exclude sources of influence outside the conversational context. Accepting that no other strategy is feasible, the first section will argue that the first step could be taken using the mothers and children described in previous chapters.

A. The emergence of group differences

The aim, then, was to see, firstly, whether children who participate in conversations like the excursive group are slower than children who participate in conversations like the recursive and discursive groups at broadening the range of nouns they provide as object names ($E < R = D$). It was to see, secondly, whether children who participate in conversations like the excursive and recursive groups are slower than children who participate in conversations like the discursive group at adopting non-names and feature combinations ($E < D$ and $R < D$). As the introduction to this chapter pointed out, these issues could be investigated following one of two approaches. The first would involve randomly assigning mothers and children to three groups and artificially creating the conversational patterns produced by the excursive, recursive and discursive groups. The children's skills at providing object names, non-names and feature combinations would be measured before and after participating in their ascribed patterns. The emergence of anticipated group differences could be taken as evidence for a causal connection between conversational experiences and the development of these skills.

Unfortunately, an investigation of this kind would intrude substantially into the lives of its mother – child participants. It would also subject children to procedures that were expected to interfere with an important area of their language development. Thus, researchers should hesitate to conduct such an investigation on ethical grounds alone. However supposing ethical scruples were overcome, the proposed investigation would also be faced with formidable practical problems. One difficulty would be guaranteeing that the three groups of mother – child pairs differed only in their conversational patterns. It could be that artificially introducing new modes of conversation would have implications for other aspects of mother – child interaction. A far more serious difficulty would arise in the actual creation of varied conversational patterns. Mothers might be persuaded to sustain their contributions, but children could not be, and the difference between the excursive and the other groups was arguably child-created. It has been stressed several times that mother-initiated exchanges beginning with requests for information were rare in the excursive group, partly because the children in this group were relatively less likely than the other children to reply to maternal requests and relatively more likely to reply to maternal provisions.

If conversational patterns of the kind produced by the three groups cannot be created artificially, the only alternative is to study children who naturally experience the conversational patterns. If predicted group differences in skill at providing information occur, further research must be conducted to overrule potentially confounding factors. Taking this for granted, it seems reasonable to ask whether the skills of the children described in previous chapters could be studied. There are obvious advantages in using an existing sample, albeit a small one, before extending the analysis to a new group. Probably the main drawback is that these children's skills at providing object names, non-names and feature combinations would have to be assessed from their contributions to the first and second recordings. Therefore, group comparison would be adequate only to the extent that the children's attempts to perform these feats during the two recordings reflected their habitual attempts. This could not be guaranteed unless the children had equal opportunities to provide object names, non-names and feature combinations during the two recordings. They were clearly provided with equal opportunities insofaras they were all recorded performing the same activity. In fact, they played with identical toys for half of each recording and similar toys for the other half. However, they may not have had equal opportunities insofaras variations in their mothers' verbosity may have given them differing chances to hold the floor. Likewise, they may have created differing changes for themselves by virtue of their own reticence. Although these possibilities cannot be overruled *a priori*, they can be controlled using measures (such as means and percentages) that compensate for overall talkativeness. Given this precaution, there seemed no reason to avoid using the children's recorded speech for estimating skill at providing object names, non-names and feature combinations. Hence, there seemed no reason to avoid using the present children to investigate group differences in the development of these skills. The three subsections of this section will explain how skill in each area was estimated, and will then summarize the results of group comparison.

(a) Naming objects

The nouns children use to name objects have been the subject of considerable research. Before proceeding to discuss the issue of particular concern, it might be interesting to review this research. Essentially, it has focused on two issues. Firstly, it has considered the kinds of object that are named, and has revealed close similarities across children. For example, both Leopold's (1939) study of one German/English bilingual girl and Nelson's (1973a) study of 18 American–English monolingual boys and girls highlight preferences for naming food, toys, animals, people, clothing, vehicles and household objects. Secondly, the research has concentrated on the kinds of object that share the same name. As has already been mentioned, this research has documented children 'overextending' or using nouns for a wider range of objects than adults would find acceptable. (6.1) is another example of overextension:

(6.1)   [Melanie (20:6) picks lorry up]
        Melanie: Car. Car.
        Mother: Is that what it is?

More recently, Anglin (1977) and Bloom (1973) have reported a corresponding tendency to 'underextend' and use nouns for what adults would regard as an unacceptably narrow range of objects. It is understandably hard to find clearcut examples of underextension in ordinary dialogue. However, the child in (6.2) evidently believes that 'feet' names a narrower set of objects than his mother does:

(6.2)   [Barry (21:18) picks up feet of model fireman]
        Mother: There's his feet.
        Barry: Not.
                It's not.
                Not feet.

With the exception of Barrett (1978), most researchers believe that people unconsciously specify sets of features that objects must share before they receive the same name. Therefore, they believe adults and children differ in their use of names because they specify different sets of features. Unfortunately, they disagree about the nature of these differences. For instance, Clark (1973, 1978), Nelson (1973a) and Nelson *et al.* (1978) believe adult specifications involve perceptual features such as shape, size and colour, together with functional features such as receptivity to certain actions. However, Clark believes that child specifications are predominantly perceptual whereas Nelson invokes functional features to some extent. As I have pointed out elsewhere (Howe, 1978), perceptual features are inherently bound up with functional ones. For example, only round objects can be rolled. Hence, attempts by researchers, such as Anglin (1977) and Nelson (1973b), to tease them apart experimentally have been rather unsatisfactory. It seems likely that the issue will eventually be regarded as irresolvable.

Fortunately, the issue does not have to be resolved for the present purpose. This is, of course, seeing whether the children in the excursive group were slower than the children in the recursive and discursive groups at broadening the range of nouns they provided as names. To make the relevant calculations, remarks that provided object names were located in the children's total corpus of speech. They numbered 27 to 214 ($M = 111.04$; SD $= 59.09$) in the first recording, and 31 to 227 ($M = 105.21$; SD $= 52.20$) in the second. Using these remarks, the number that provided different names was calculated for every child. It varied from 8 to 48 ($M = 28.79$: SD $= 13.12$) in the first recording, and 20 to 90 ($M = 40.00$; SD $= 17.94$) in the second. In accordance with the findings of Leopold (1939) and Nelson (1973a), the children generally provided the names of ordinary objects. However, they occasionally mentioned quite esoteric things, such as 'Daffodil', 'Helicopter', 'Llama' and 'Stethoscope'. To give some idea of the range, the Appendix (p. 143) lists every different object name provided by the children whose conversations represented the three groups in Chapters 3 and 4.

The most straightforward measure of nouns for naming objects would be the total number of different names provided for objects. However as the introduction to this section pointed out, this could be misleading if the children had different opportunities to name objects. Hence, it seemed desirable to use the percentages of different names in total names provided for objects. These percentages were duly calculated and are presented in Table 6.1. Next, the mean and standard deviation percentages were computed from both recordings for the three groups. They are shown in Fig. 6.1.

Table 6.1. *Percentage of different object names*

Name (group in brackets)	First recording			Second recording		
	No. of names	No. of diff. names	% of diff. names	No. of names	No. of diff. names	% of diff. names
Alan (E)	77	23	29.87	88	23	26.14
Barry (D)	114	34	29.82	31	22	70.97
Caroline (E)	90	26	28.89	94	36	38.30
Daniel (D)	135	32	23.70	48	24	50.00
Eileen (R)	60	13	21.67	125	52	41.60
Faye (R)	33	19	57.58	109	35	32.11
Graham (D)	202	26	12.87	174	69	39.66
Hayley (R)	134	45	33.58	89	47	52.81
Ian (R)	74	29	39.19	62	35	56.45
Jason (R)	27	8	29.63	202	90	44.55
Kevin (D)	159	46	28.93	80	46	57.50
Lucy (R)	50	12	24.00	44	23	52.27
Melanie (R)	211	29	13.74	113	41	36.28
Nicola (D)	44	14	31.82	163	73	44.79
Oliver (E)	167	46	27.54	167	44	26.35
Philip (R)	42	9	21.43	91	26	28.57
Richard (E)	187	45	24.06	62	27	43.55
Sally (D)	214	48	22.43	162	54	33.33
Tom (D)	87	38	43.68	45	22	48.89
Ursula (D)	126	48	38.10	61	24	39.34
Virginia (D)	83	26	31.33	127	48	37.80
Wayne (E)	158	17	10.76	227	29	12.78
Yvonne (D)	153	41	26.80	97	50	51.55
Zoe (D)	38	17	44.74	64	20	31.25

One-way analysis of variance revealed no significant group differences in these percentages for the first recording ($F = 0.63$; df $= 2/21$; Not significant). However, there was a significant difference for the second recording percentages ($F = 3.81$; df $= 2/21$; $p < 0.05$). Subsequent analysis by t-test showed that the mean for the excursive group was almost significantly lower than the mean for the recursive group ($t = 2.13$; df $= 11$; $p < 0.10$). It was significantly lower than the mean for the discursive group ($t = 2.72$; df $= 2/21$; $p < 0.02$). However, the means for the recursive and discursive groups did not differ significantly from each other ($t = 0.54$; df $= 17$; Not significant). Thus, these results do provide some evidence that the children in the excursive group were slower than the other children at broadening their repertoire of nouns for naming objects ($E < R = D$).

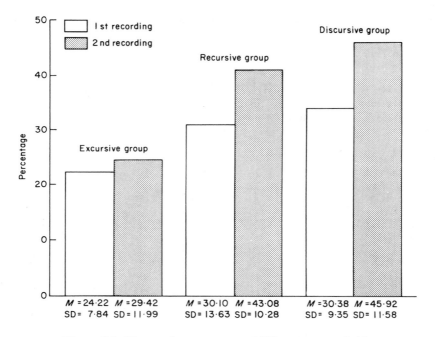

Figure 6.1. *Changes in percentages of different names of objects*

(b) Mentioning non-names

The second relevant aspect of providing information was mentioning features other than names or non-names. Of course, non-names include a wide variety of features, such as quantities, properties, owners, recipients, locations and actions. It might be argued that these features vary in conceptual difficulty. Indeed, Greenfield and Smith (1976) and Wells (1974) have made exactly this point. If they are correct and if, say, locations are conceptually more difficult than actions, it might be misleading to treat children whose non-names contained locations as equivalent to children whose non-names contained only actions. Fortunately however, the evidence on variations in conceptual difficulty is extremely ambiguous. For instance, the work of Greenfield and Smith (1976) implies that features such as locations and properties are more difficult than actions or recipients. Despite terminological differences, the work of Wells (1974) implies the reverse. These inconsistencies may reflect individual or, indeed, cross-cultural differences. Alternatively, they may reflect the ambiguities inherent in early speech.

In earlier papers (Howe, 1976, 1977, 1979), I have suggested that it is usually clear whether or not children are naming the object of their action or gaze. It is also usually clear whether or not children are mentioning quantities, properties or actions, since these features are normally marked by particular words. This was why the percentages of child-initiated exchanges beginning with remarks about names, properties and actions could be presented with some confidence in Chapters 3 and 4. However, it is almost always unclear whether children are mentioning some of the other features until their speech becomes quite sophisticated. For example, it is unclear in the absence of prepositions whether 'Kevin' in (6.3) is meant as owner, recipient, location or, indeed, 'generally related object', despite reasonably detailed non-verbal information:

(6.3)   [Kevin (20:21) holds cup]
     Kevin: Tea. Kevin.
     Mother: Tea for Kevin.
     Kevin: Tea Kevin.
     Mother: Yes, here you are, Kevin.

Of course, Kevin's mother was convinced that 'Kevin' was meant as a recipient, and it has been argued that mothers' interpretations can be used in classification. This is because mothers have been credited with special insight into their children's meanings. The previous chapter gave examples that should challenge this; (6.4) should reinforce them:

(6.4)   [Kevin (20:21) has removed xylophone notes]
     Kevin: Off. Off. Off. Off.
     Mother: You can't take any more off.
     Kevin: Off. Off.
     Mother: Do you want to put it on again?
     Kevin: Off. Off.
     Mother: That goes on here.

	Look there, now it's 'on'.
Kevin:	Off. Off. Off. Off.
Mother:	It's 'on', Kevin.
	Can you say 'on'? 'On'.
Kevin:	Off. Off. Off.
	Took it off.

Since the various non-names may not appear in a set order, and since they cannot always be differentiated empirically, it was decided to concentrate on overall use of non-names. Again, it seemed desirable to assess this with a ratio measure to compensate for possible differences in opportunities to talk. The measure adopted was the percentage of remarks about non-names in all remarks that provided information. In order to take this measure, remarks that provided information were divided into those that did and did not simply name the object of ongoing action or gaze. Once this had been done, the wisdom of not discriminating different kinds of non-names became clear. As the lists in the Appendix (p. 145) show, some features could be unambiguously classified as quantities, properties, owners, locations and so on. For example, remarks such as 'There more over there', 'That hot', 'Mine', 'In bath' and 'Barking' seemed relatively clear-cut. However, the number of uncertain cases meant that any attempt to place every remark into these categories would have produced utterly arbitrary percentages. The simple distinction between names and non-names elicited far less ambiguity. Thus, the percentages of remarks about non-names were calculated with some confidence.

The percentages for every child in both recordings are shown in Table 6.2 and the means and standard deviations for the three groups are shown in Fig. 6.2. One-way analyses of variance produced no significant group differences in the first recording ($F = 0.44$; df $= 2/21$; Not significant) but significant group differences in the second recording ($F = 4.43$; df $= 2/21$; $p < 0.025$). Further analysis by *t*-test revealed that in the second recording the mean difference between the excursive and recursive groups was far from statistically significant ($t = 1.17$; df $= 11$; Not significant). The mean difference between the excursive and discursive groups was considerably higher, but still not statistically significant ($t = 1.32$; df $= 14$; Not significant). However, the mean difference between the recursive and discursive groups was highly significant ($t = 2.96$; df $= 17$; $p < 0.01$). This amounts to some evidence that the children in the discursive group were quicker than the children in the excursive and recursive groups to introduce features other than names (E < D and R < D).

Table 6.2. *Percentage of remarks about non-names*

Name (group in brackets)	First recording			Second recording		
	No. of provisions	No. of non-names	% of non-names	No. of provisions	No. of non-names	% of non-names
Alan (E)	100	23	23.00	133	45	33.83
Barry (D)	152	38	25.00	75	44	58.67
Caroline (E)	120	30	25.00	151	57	37.75
Daniel (D)	157	22	14.01	75	27	36.00
Eileen (R)	69	9	13.04	153	28	18.30
Faye (R)	44	11	25.00	163	54	33.13
Graham (D)	204	2	0.98	253	79	31.23
Hayley (R)	156	22	14.10	134	45	33.58
Ian (R)	146	72	49.32	146	84	57.53
Jason (R)	35	8	22.86	228	26	11.40
Kevin (D)	200	41	20.50	206	126	61.17
Lucy (R)	61	11	18.03	90	46	51.11
Melanie (R)	265	54	20.38	150	37	24.67
Nicola (D)	49	5	10.20	277	114	41.16
Oliver (E)	186	19	10.22	347	180	51.87
Philip (R)	82	40	48.78	125	34	27.20
Richard (E)	348	161	46.26	132	70	53.03
Sally (D)	261	47	18.01	307	145	47.23
Tom (D)	109	22	20.18	132	87	65.91
Ursula (D)	138	12	8.70	120	59	49.17
Virginia (D)	158	75	47.47	214	87	40.65
Wayne (E)	164	6	3.66	315	88	27.94
Yvonne (D)	178	25	14.04	264	167	63.26
Zoe (D)	66	28	42.42	151	87	57.62

(c) Using feature combinations

Clearly, remarks that provide more than one feature of an object or 'feature combinations' are going to be a subset of remarks that provide non-names.

The question is whether the subset of feature combinations shows the same group differences (E < D and R < D) as the overall set of non-names. To answer this question, it was necessary to decide upon a measure of skill at providing feature combinations. One possibility was the mean number of features mentioned in remarks that provided information. However, the first recording produced precisely three remarks that mentioned more than two features, and the second recording produced 28. In the light of this, it seemed reasonable to create some symmetry with the other measures and use the percentage of remarks providing information that mentioned more than one feature.

Again, it would have been a mistake to classify the types of feature. The children certainly produced many unambiguous instances of the combinations described by Bloom (1970), Bowerman (1973), Brown (1973), Schlesinger (1971) and Slobin (1970). For example, 'Yellow lorry' and 'Wrong page' seemed clear instances of property plus name; 'She my dolly' and 'It's a man's hat' of owner plus name; 'Lion in the house' and 'Pants on dolly' of location plus name; and 'A tiger coming' and 'Cow won't go' of action plus name. However as the list in the Appendix (p. 145) shows, there were many

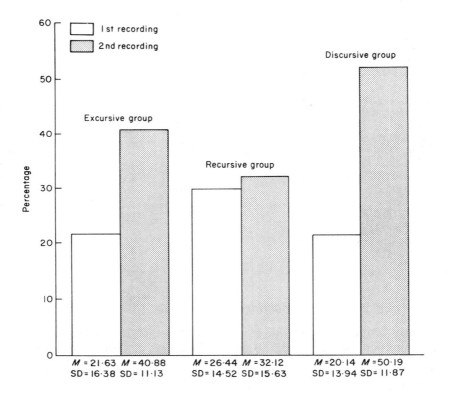

Figure 6.2. *Changes over time in percentage of non-names*

combinations that no amount of contextual information could disambiguate. This was particularly true of sequences containing two nouns, such as 'Picture daddy', 'Baby man' and 'Cow doggie'. Thus, the simple percentages of informative remarks that mentioned more than one feature was used. The individual percentages from both recordings are given in Table

6.3, and the means and standard deviations for the three groups appear in Fig. 6.3. There were no group differences on a one-way analysis of variance in the first recording ($F = 0.18$; df $= 2/21$; Not significant) but statistically significant group differences in the second recording ($F = 7.97$; df $= 2/21$; $p < 0.01$). Subsequent analyses by t-test revealed that the mean for the discursive group was significantly higher than the means for the excursive ($t = 2.24$; df $= 14$; $p < 0.05$) and recursive ($t = 3.89$; df $= 17$; $p < 0.01$) groups. There was no significant mean difference between the excursive and recursive groups ($t = 1.06$; df $= 11$; Not significant). The overall superiority of the children in the discursive group was exactly what the model outlined earlier would predict.

Table 6.3. *Percentage of feature combinations*

Name (group in brackets)	First recording			Second recording		
	No. of provisions	No. of feature combinations	% of feature combinations	No. of provisions	No. of feature combinations	% of feature combinations
Alan (E)	100	13	13.00	133	32	24.06
Barry (D)	152	13	8.55	75	11	14.67
Caroline (E)	120	13	10.83	151	15	9.93
Daniel (D)	157	6	3.82	75	16	21.33
Eileen (R)	69	2	2.90	153	16	10.46
Faye (R)	44	4	9.09	163	21	12.88
Graham (D)	204	2	0.98	253	33	13.04
Hayley (R)	156	6	3.85	134	13	9.70
Ian (R)	146	15	10.27	146	18	12.33
Jason (R)	35	0	0	228	5	2.19
Kevin (D)	200	7	3.50	206	66	32.04
Lucy (R)	61	7	11.48	90	13	14.44
Melanie (R)	265	5	1.89	150	21	14.00
Nicola (D)	49	0	0	277	55	19.86
Oliver (E)	186	4	2.15	347	82	23.63
Philip (R)	82	0	0	125	9	7.20
Richard (E)	348	11	3.16	132	21	15.91
Sally (D)	261	16	6.13	307	57	18.57
Tom (D)	109	4	3.67	132	43	32.58
Ursula (D)	138	2	1.45	120	35	29.17
Virginia (D)	158	15	9.49	214	35	16.36
Wayne (E)	164	1	0.61	315	4	1.27
Yvonne (D)	178	15	8.43	264	101	38.26
Zoe (D)	66	3	4.55	151	44	29.14

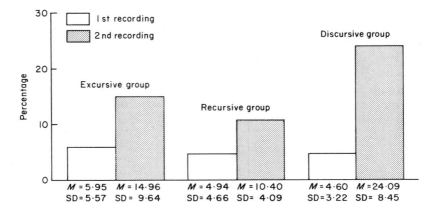

Figure 6.3. *Changes over time in percentage of feature combinations*

B. The alternative sources of group difference

All in all, the results were largely in agreement with suggestions made in the previous chapter about the effect of mother – child conversation on child language development. In that chapter, it was argued that mother-initiated exchanges beginning with requests for information should motivate children to develop their skill at providing object names, non-names and feature combinations. Mother-initiated exchanges beginning with provisions of information should not motivate the development of these aspects of providing information. The children in the excursive group differed from the children in the discursive group only in their lesser experience of mother-initiated exchanges beginning with requests for information. In agreement with the suggestions, they were significantly or nearly significantly slower than the children in the discursive group at developing their skill at providing names, non-names and feature combinations.

In addition, the previous chapter suggested that child-initiated exchanges ending with minimal replies should yield data relevant to the expansion of nouns for naming objects. Child-initiated exchanges ending with extended replies should yield data relevant to both the expansion of nouns for naming objects and the provision of non-names and feature combinations. The children in the recursive group differed from the children in the discursive group only in their lesser experience of child-initiated exchanges ending with

extended replies. Once more in agreement with the suggestions, they developed their skill at providing object names at roughly the same pace. Moreover, they were significantly slower in developing their skill at providing
non-names and feature combinations. The children in the recursive group
differed from the children in the excursive group in their greater experience
of mother-initiated exchanges beginning with requests for information and
their lesser experience of child-initiated exchanges ending with extended
replies. Hence in relation to the children in the excursive group, they had
both the motivation and the information to develop their skill at providing
object names. They had the motivation, but not the information, to develop
their skill at providing non-names and feature combinations. Indeed, the
children in the excursive group had more information about these skills.
Overall, the children in the recursive group should develop their skill at
naming objects faster than the children in the excursive group. They did.
Their relative speed at introducing non-names and feature combinations
could not be predicted, since the comparative importance of motivation and
information could not be assessed. In fact, the children in the recursive
group did not differ from the children in the excursive group in developing
these skills.

Although largely in agreement with suggestions made in the previous
chapter, the results cannot be taken as conclusive evidence for these suggestions. It is possible that the groups differed in other, hitherto unrecognized,
respects that could also have caused the differences outlined in the previous
section. The present section will take a few steps towards assessing this
possibility. It will try to specify the most plausible alternative sources of
group difference, dividing them into those outside the children's linguistic
environment and those within. This section will also indicate where the
contribution of alternative sources can be estimated from existing data and
where further research is needed. It will show that no source which could be
adequately investigated was likely to influence the group differences.

(a) Outside the linguistic environment

The first of these alternative sources lies in the inbuilt capacities to acquire
language that many writers have attributed to young children. As pointed
out in Chapter 1, there has been some debate about the generality of these
capacities. For instance, Lenneberg (1964, 1967) and McNeill (1966a,
1966b) have suggested they are specific to language, whereas Sinclair (1969,
1971, 1973) has claimed they are common to all conceptual activities.
Proponents of both specific and general points of view have suggested that
children are differentially endowed with capacities for language acquisition,
allowing the possibility that such individual differences covaried with the

groups. If they covaried, they could have caused the group differences. Rather weak evidence against the possibility of covariance can be inferred from Table 6.4 which shows the sex, birth order and social class of the children in the three groups. Using data from Table 6.4, Fisher Exact Probability Tests (Siegel, 1956) revealed no significant group differences in sex, birth order or social class. Since sex has been associated with specific

Table 6.4. *Sex, birth order and social class distribution of the three groups*

Group	Sex		
	Male	Female	Total
Excursive	4	1	5
Recursive	3	5	8
Discursive	5	6	11
Total	12	12	24

Group	Birth order		
	First born[a]	Later born	Total
Excursive	2	3	5
Recursive	5	3	8
Discursive	6	5	11
Total	13	11	24

Group	Social class		
	Working class	Middle class	Total
Excursive	2	3	5
Recursive	5	3	8
Discursive	4	7	11
Total	11	13	24

[a]Both twins are counted as first-born although Tom was literally the eldest by 12 hours.

capacities for language by Buffery and Gray (1972), and birth order and social class have been associated with general conceptual abilities by countless writers, these results could suggest that the children in the three groups were unlikely to differ in any inbuilt capacities for language. Quite conclusive evidence against the influence of inbuilt capacities, even if they did covary with the groups, can be inferred from the group differences themselves, particularly the finding that the discursive group exceeded the excursive group on three measures and the recursive group on two. As inbuilt capacities for language acquisition are meant to pervade all aspects of the process, they could not account for variations in the pattern of group differences. In other words, it is in the nature of the results to dispel inbuilt capacities as a contributory factor.

A second potential source of influence is non-linguistic experiences. Children are unlikely to learn the names, let alone the other features, of objects they have not experienced directly in their lives or indirectly through pictures. However, the influence of non-linguistic experiences can be overruled by arguments similar to those presented in the previous paragraph. Firstly, it can be argued that non-linguistic experiences were unlikely to vary across the groups. Chapter 2 reported little variance in the general routine of the 24 children. Casual inspection indicated little variation in the more specific aspects of these routines, such as the particular toys played with and the particular foods eaten. Moreover, work reported by Maccoby and Jacklin (1975) and Smilansky (1968) suggests that any variations that did exist were likely to be associated with sex and/or social class. Data have just been presented to show that the three groups were not sex- or class-related. Secondly, it can also be argued that non-linguistic experiences were unlikely to cause the group differences, even if they did vary across the groups. It is hard to imagine that any non-linguistic experience which benefitted object naming would not also benefit the appreciation of other factors. Yet, that would have to happen if the varied pattern of group differences were to be explained by non-linguistic experiences.

(b) Within the linguistic environment

Thus, two considerations lower the likelihood of factors in outside the linguistic environment causing the group differences. In the first place, the most obvious of these factors seemed unlikely to covary with the groups. In the second place, they seemed unlikely to cause a varied pattern of differences even if they did covary with the groups. Turning to alternative linguistic factors, somewhat different considerations have to be borne in mind. The potentially linguistic factors fall into two groups: other factors that could have motivated the children to develop the relevant aspects of providing information, and other factors that could have shown them how to develop. With respect to the first group, it is hard to think of candidates beyond conversational exchanges initiated by the mothers (and of course other people) that begin with requests for information. The previous chapter suggested that child-initiated exchanges where other people misunderstand the function of children's remarks should motivate children to develop certain aspects of performing the function in question. Thus, child-initiated exchanges where remarks intended to provide information were perceived as performing some other function (presumably directing behaviour) should motivate children to develop some aspects of using language to provide information. (6.4) contained several examples of such exchanges; (6.5) probably contains another:

(6.5)   [Faye (23:18) turns block]
       Faye: Ball.
                On a house.
       Mother: Do you want the house there?
       Faye: Uh?
                House.
                That. That.
                That house.
                That on house that one.

However, these exchanges seem unlikely to motivate the aspects of current interest. Since the ambiguity of children's remarks is primarily a function of their ill formedness, these exchanges seem more likely to motivate the use of better formed expressions. In addition to this, it might be argued that requests for information should motivate children to develop the relevant aspect of providing information whether or not these requests receive replies. This seems rather implausible. It would mean that children were motivated to learn skills needed for a communicative role that they did not necessarily wish to perform. Whatever its truth however, data have already been presented to show that group differences in mothers' requests at least, were fairly small in the first recording and non-existent in the second.

So far the analysis of alternative sources of group difference has proved easier than expected. The contribution of factors in outside the linguistic environment can be more or less excluded without further research. The contribution of other motivational factors can be excluded if there are no other sources of motivation. Unfortunately, the contribution of alternative information about using language to provide information cannot be so readily excluded. Such information is potentially available in every provision of information overheard by children. It is arguably also available in remarks used for most other communicative functions. The contribution of alternative information from the mothers can be assessed using present data. The contribution of alternative information from other people must remain the subject of further research. To make some assessment of whether alternative information from the mothers might be influencing present group differences, the mothers' total speech was subjected to the same analysis as the children's had been in the previous section. First, the percentages of different names in total names provided for objects were calculated, and one-way analyses of variance were used to detect group differences. There were no significant differences in either the first (F = 1.18; df = 2/21; Not significant) or the second (F = 0.50; df = 2/21; Not significant) recordings. Then, the percentages of non-names in total remarks providing information were calculated. One-way analyses of variance showed no significant differences between the groups in either the first (F = 0.24; df = 2/21; Not significant) or the second (F = 1.87; df = 2/21; Not significant) recordings. Finally, the percentages of feature combinations in total remarks providing information were calculated and again the groups were compared on one-way analyses of variance. Once more, there were no significant differences in either the first (F = 2.38; df = 2/21; Not significant) or the second (F = 0.21; df = 2/21; Not significant) recordings. Taken together, these results indicate that alternative information from the mothers' speech was not influencing the present group differences.

7 Some Further Questions about Variations in Mother – Child Conversation

The past five chapters have described a study into the nature and significance of mother – child conversation. The study was based on recordings of 24 mother – child pairs who were videotaped on two occasions while they played with toys in their homes. On the first occasion, the children were aged 20–22 months, and on the second they were aged 23–25 months. Transcripts of these recordings were scrutinized for 'conversational exchanges', that is exchanges where the first speaker addressed a request or provision of information to the second speaker, and the second speaker addressed a minimal or extended reply to the first speaker. Only four of the eight possible types of exchange occurred with any frequency in mother – child conversation. They were:

1. Mother-initiated exchanges beginning with requests for information and ending with minimal replies.
2. Mother-initiated exchanges beginning with provisions of information and ending with minimal replies.
3. Child-initiated exchanges beginning with provisions of information and ending with minimal replies.
4. Child-initiated exchanges beginning with provisions of information and ending with extended replies.

However although these types of exchange sometimes occurred frequently, they did not invariably do so. Five mother – child pairs, who were designated the excursive group, rarely engaged in mother-initiated exchanges beginning with requests for information. Eight mother – child pairs, who were designated the recursive group, rarely engaged in child-initiated exchanges ending with extended replies. Only the 11 mother – child pairs, who were designated the discursive group frequently engaged in all four types of exchange.

The importance of this variability became apparent once the developmental implications of the four types of exchange were discussed. As a result of this discussion, it was suggested that mother-initiated exchanges beginning with requests for information might motivate children to provide more varied object names, more features other than object names, or 'non-names, and more combinations of features in single remarks, or 'feature combinations'. Mother-initiated exchanges beginning with provisions of information should have no impact on motivation to develop these aspects of providing information. Child-initiated exchanges ending with minimal replies might yield data relevant to the range of nouns and the well formedness of speech used to provide object names. Child-initiated exchanges ending with extended replies might yield data relevant to the provision both of object names and well formed speech and of non-names and feature combinations. If these suggestions proved correct, the variability in mother – child conversation would mean that children derive differing degrees of assistance from their conversational experiences. Because of their limited experience with mother-initiated exchanges beginning with requests for information, the children in the excursive group should be less motivated than the children in the recursive and discursive groups to develop their skill at providing information about object names, non-names and feature combinations. Because of their limited experience with child-initiated exchanges ending with extended replies, the children in the recursive group should be less informed than the children in the excursive and discursive groups about the provision of non-names and feature combinations, but equally informed about the provision of object names and the use of well formed expressions.

If the children differ only in their conversational experiences, this differential assistance should show itself through group differences in using language to provide information. It might or might not show itself through group differences in using language to perform other communicative functions. The children in the excursive group should be slower than the children in the recursive and discursive groups at expanding the range of names they provide for objects. The children in the excursive and recursive groups should be slower than the children in the discursive group at providing information about non-names and feature combinations. Subsequent analysis revealed group differences that were largely in agreement with these predictions. The children in the excursive group were slower than the children in the recursive and discursive groups at broadening the range of names they provided for objects. The children in the excursive and recursive groups were slower than the children in the discursive group at incorporating non-names and feature combinations into the information they provided. However despite being in agreement with its predictions, these group differences could not be taken as *prima facie* evidence for the present ideas about how mother – child conversation assists child language development. The differences could have been caused by factors outside the conversational context. Accordingly, the previous chapter tried to specify these factors and assess their contribution wherever possible. In its second endeavour, the previous chapter found no compelling evidence for confounding factors. However, it could not adequately investigate every potential interference. It ended by calling for further research to clarify the issue.

The upshot of this research would be to strengthen or weaken the belief that observed variations in mother-initiated exchanges beginning with requests for information, and child-initiated exchanges ending with extended replies, produce variations in skill at providing object names, non-names and feature combinations. Strengthening this belief would constitute support for certain aspects of the present model. Specifically, it would endorse the view that mother-initiated exchanges beginning with requests for information motivate children to provide new names, non-names and feature combinations. It would also suggest that child-initiated exchanges ending with minimal replies inform children about providing new names, whereas child-initiated exchanges ending with extended replies inform children about providing new names, non-names and feature combinations. It would not resolve the issue of whether the two types of child-initiated exchange inform children about well formed expressions for providing information. Of course, strengthening the aforementioned belief would do more than simply support a theoretical model. It would also provide a final answer to the underlying research question, namely whether mother – child conversation facilitates language development. This answer would claim that mother – child conversation helps all children to some extent. However, children who participate in conversations like the excursive group receive less help than children who participate in conversations like the recursive group, who in turn receive less help than children who participate in conversations like the discursive group.

Answering the original research question should not of course terminate interest in mother – child conversation. Rather, it should stimulate research into new questions that arise directly out of the answer given. Two such questions immediately spring to mind. The first concerns the reasons why the excursive and recursive groups held conversations that were apparently less than ideal. The second was raised and temporarily glossed over in the previous chapter. It concerns the speed with which children in the excursive and recursive groups developed skill at performing functions other than providing information. Although seemingly distinct, the two questions are in fact quite closely related. It would be impossible to teach mothers and children to hold conversations like the discursive group without knowing why they preferred conversations like the excursive and recursive groups. It would be undesirable to teach them without knowing the extent of disadvantages caused by conversations like the excursive and recursive groups. Partly because of their practical implications and partly because of their general theoretical interest, this chapter will discuss these questions.

A. The origins of variations in mother – child conversation

At first sight, the practical implications of the present research seem clear. Mothers and children who naturally tend to other conversational patterns should be encouraged to emulate the mothers and children in the discursive group. On further reflection, the situation becomes more complicated. Irrespective of desirability, it would be impossible to encourage any mother and child to adopt the conversational pattern of the discursive group without knowing why they avoided this style in the first place. As a first step towards clarifying this issue, this section will propose reasons why some mothers and children fell into the excursive and recursive rather than discursive groups.

(a) Excursive v discursive

The basic difference between the excursive and discursive groups was their respective percentages of mother-initiated exchanges beginning with requests for information. Such exchanges were virtually unknown in the excursive group, but quite common in the discursive group. The purely statistical reasons for this difference were presented in Chapters 3 and 4. As those chapters made clear, the difference was apparent in both the first and the second recordings. However in the first recording, it arose partly because the mothers in the excursive group produced proportionately fewer requests for information than the mothers in the discursive group. It arose also because the children in the excursive group replied to proportionately fewer requests and proportionately more provisions of information than the children in the discursive group. In the second recording, it arose simply because the children in the excursive group replied to proportionately fewer requests and proportionately more provisions of information than the children in the discursive group. The absence of difference between the mothers was due to the proportions of maternal requests increasing slightly in the excursive group and decreasing slightly in the discursive group.

These results seem open to at least two interpretations. Firstly, the recordings may have been made towards the end of a period when the percentage of requests for information from the mothers in the excursive group was increasing from a very low level. At the start of that hypothetical period, the children in the excursive group would have been faced with two alternatives: replying to provisions of information or no conversation at all. Having chosen the first alternative, they may have continued in their habitual roles even when increases in maternal requests meant they could adopt other roles. Such rigidity would explain why they replied to proportionately fewer requests and proportionately more provisions of information than the children in the discursive group during both recordings. The second interpretation views the percentage of requests for information from the mothers as largely irrelevant. It proposes that the children in the excursive group were temperamentally inclined to the passive role of acknowledging information which their mothers provide, as in (7.1):

(7.1)   [Oliver (23:19) opens door of car]
        Mother: And that's the driving wheel.
        Oliver: Driving wheel.

The children in the discursive group were temperamentally inclined to the more active role of providing new information in response to their mothers' requests, as in (7.2):

(7.2)   [Ursula (21:3) and mother look at pictures]
        Mother: What's that picture?
        Ursula: Beetle.

Hence, the children in the excursive group would have replied to proportionately fewer requests and proportionately more provisions of information than the children in the discursive group, even if their mothers had not differed in the first recording.

To evaluate these interpretations, it would be necessary to record children who were known to be at the very beginnings of conversation. The second interpretation would be supported if these children showed differential response tendencies regardless of their mother's requests and provisions of information. The first would be supported if the children's response tendencies were correlated with their mothers' speech style. Should the first interpretation be supported, the implications for potentially excursive mothers who wished to emulate the discursive group would be clear. They should increase their initial level of requests for information and sustain their initial level of extended replies. They could do this by adding requests for information to extended replies, as in (7.3), or by using requests for information as extended replies, as in (7.4):

(7.3)   [Sally (20:8) puts lorry down]
        Sally: Lorry.
        Mother: Yes, here you are.

That's part of the lorry.
What else is in here?

(7.4) [Kevin (20:21) and mother look at book]
    Kevin: Car.
    Mother: It's a pram, isn't it?
               What goes inside a pram?
    Kevin: Baby.

Of course, the ease with which mothers could turn on new speech styles would depend on their attachment to old ones. Thus, it seems important to discuss why the mothers in the excursive group did in fact use fewer requests and more provisions of information than the mothers in the discursive group. One clue comes from the demands that requests and provisions of information place on their addressees. Requests for information do not only demand responses from their addressees. As pointed out in Chapter 5, they require responses that spontaneously provide requested information. Provisions of information, however, do not necessarily require any response. When responses occur, they can be as limited as grunts of acknowledgement. This suggests that mothers will not request information until they know their children are capable of replying. Before this, they will tend only to provide information. If this is true, it means that the mothers in the excursive group differed from the mothers in the discursive group because they were slower to realize their children had learned to cope with requests for information. In other words, they were less sensitive.

Now the most direct evidence for this suggestion would come from asking mothers when their children learned to cope with requests for information. Answers from the mothers in the excursive group should be more conservative and less accurate than answers from mothers in the discursive group. In the absence of such direct evidence, the suggestion can be tested indirectly via some of its implications. Firstly, the suggestion implies that the mothers in the excursive group would eventually become like the mothers in the discursive group. Some support for this comes from the finding that the mothers produced similar percentages of requests for information in the second recording. Secondly, the suggestion implies that the mothers in the discursive group must have once been like the mothers in the excursive group. Some anecdotal support for this comes from comments made by Snow (1977a) and from the mother in (7.5), who was not placed in the excursive group on the basis of her exchanges with an older child:

(7.5) [Mother tries to feed Deborah (3.2)]
    Mother: You're cheeky.
               You're teasing me, aren't you?
               You're a teaser. You're a teaser.

You're a teaser.
You're a teaser.
[Deborah gurgles]
Mother: You're not drinking it.
You're just mucking about.
You're teasing. You're teasing.
You're teasing Mummy.

The suggestion derives more rigorous support from Ringler's (1978) study of mothers' speech to children aged 10–13 months. Ringler found that questions rarely appeared at this stage, whereas statements were quite common. Of course, questions are not synonymous with requests for information, and statements are not synonymous with provisions of information. Nevertheless, Ringler's results are compatible with the suggestion that other mothers talk like the mothers in the excursive group while interacting with very young children.

The idea that the mothers in the excursive group were fairly insensitive to their children's conversational skills raises the question of whether they were equally insensitive in other areas. The work of Broen (1972), Phillips (1973), Remick (1976), Snow (1972) and its tabulation by Snow (1977b) has already been mentioned. This work shows that mothers make certain structural modifications when speaking to 2-year-olds that could facilitate grammatical development. Phillips (1973) also analysed mothers' speech to 8-month-olds, discovering that many of the structural modifications were missing. Her finding suggests that these modifications will not appear until mothers think their children can appreciate them. Like requests for information, their usage seems to be a question of maternal sensitivity. In the light of points made earlier, it would be interesting to see whether mothers who fall into the excursive group are slower to make these structural modifications as well.

Before becoming too involved with the mothers, it would be as well to remember that the difference between the excursive and discursive groups need not have originated in maternal speech at all. It might also reflect temperamental differences between the children. Should the evidence point to this interpretation, the implications for mothers will be less clear-cut. The implications depend on whether temperamental differences reflect earlier experiences or biological predispositions. If the former, mothers may be able to encourage temperamental activity by some yet unformulated non-linguistic method. If the latter, there is probably little mothers can do to enhance replies to requests for information. Unfortunately, the work of Kagan (1971) suggests biological bases to temperamental differences are not totally implausible. Kagan tested 180 children on various developmental measures when these children were 4, 8, 13 and 27 months old. One measure was concerned with the 'tempo' of play, that is the number of activity changes within an observation period. High tempo must reflect what has been called 'active temperament' in this chapter. Interestingly, Kagan found that levels of tempo were reasonably stable across observation sessions, suggesting, though by no means proving, an underlying biological factor. Stronger evidence would come from correlations between perinatal activity levels and subsequent conversational patterns.

A temperamental interpretation of the differences between the excursive and discursive groups would have interesting theoretical implications. For instance, it would entail a wider conception of what children bring to the task of language learning. As a result of Braine's (1963) demonstrations that children produce novel combinations, such as 'Goed', 'Mouses', 'A shoes', 'There come milkman there' and 'I me draw pussy cat eyes', it has generally been accepted that children bring rules for restructuring linguistic input. As has been pointed out elsewhere, some writers think these rules are specific to language, whereas others think they are common to all conceptual activities. However, few writers have considered, let alone acknowledged, that children might bring more than these rules. If the differences between the excursive and discursive groups have temperamental origins, this point must be conceded. It must be accepted that children are not only equipped with rules for restructuring linguistic input, but they are also equipped with temperaments that influence their conversational behaviour and ultimately their willingness to learn from linguistic input.

(b) Recursive v discursive

Discussing the difference between the excursive and discursive groups has been complicated by one major uncertainty. This was whether the difference was initiated by the mothers or the children. No such uncertainty enters into any discussion of the difference between the recursive and discursive groups. The main difference between these groups resulted from the mothers in the recursive group producing far fewer extended replies than the mothers in the discursive group. Hence, the difference between the recursive and discursive groups is undeniably mother-created. The central question is why the mothers created it. One answer is that the mothers in the recursive and discursive groups responded differently to semantic inadequacies in their children's speech. Noting that their children's speech was more or less restricted to naming objects, the mothers in the recursive group made names the primary topic of conversation. For these mothers, conversation meant playing what Brown (1957) has called 'the original word game'. Like the mother in (7.6), they used *wh*-questions to request names and then gave evaluative and/or corrective replies:

(7.6) [Faye (23:18) plays with jigsaw]
    Mother: Do you know what this is?
    Faye: Uhm shop, town.
    Mother: Town!
              And what's this?
    Faye: 'O' that.
    Mother: It's an 'O'!
              It's a ball.

The mothers in the discursive group also noted that their children's speech was virtually limited to naming objects. Moreover, they also accepted that inadequate names must be corrected. However, they were unwilling to make names the primary topic of conversation. Rather, they decided to take responsibility for providing alternative topics. Like the mother in (7.7), they wove their children's names into complex strings of topic change, thereby producing extended replies:

(7.7) [Mother and Kevin (23:27) look at pictures]
    Mother: This is a supermarket, isn't it?
              Sometimes we go to the supermarket to do our shopping.
              What's that little girl got?
    Kevin: Basket.
    Mother: The little girl's getting something out of her basket, isn't she?
              What's she getting?
    Kevin: Tissues.

To check this interpretation, it would be necessary to conduct rather sensitive interviews with mothers from the recursive and discursive groups. If these interviews showed it to be correct, it would mean that the differences between the recursive and discursive groups did not reflect differences in maternal sensitivity. The mothers in the two groups would be equally aware of limitations in their children's speech. They would, of course, also be aware of their children's ability to reply to requests for information. Instead, the difference would reflect disparate conclusions about the implications of these limitations. Moreover, these disparate conclusions would probably reflect conscious decisions backed up by reasoned argument. They would be very resistant to change. It is easy to imagine the mothers in the recursive group saying there was no point in mentioning anything but names because their children would never understand. Indeed, it is possible to imagine them claiming the psycholinguistic literature supports their view. In fact, it does nothing of the kind. In implying that mothers' speech to young children should be modified, the psycholinguistic literature does not mean it should be reduced to the children's own level. Rather, it should always remain somewhat ahead. For instance, Moerk (1974) believes that mothers' speech is helpful, not because it contains the same number of syllables as children's, but because it contains slightly more.

B. The importance of variations in mother – child conversation

The previous section has discussed the origins and inevitability of variations in mother – child conversation. It has theorized about possible origins, and suggested how they might be investigated empirically. It has explained how entrenched the variations would be given proposed origins. It started by considering the origins of differences between the excursive and discursive groups. Given the data presented in Chapters 3 and 4, it could not decide whether the differences originated with the mothers or the children. If with the mothers, the differences could simply reflect variations in the sensitivity of mothers who held similar opinions about their conversational role. If with the children, the differences could be deeply and resistently rooted in early experiences or biological predispositions. The previous section then considered the origins of differences between the recursive and discursive groups. Although these differences were indubitably mother-created, they might be less 'accidental' than any mother-created differences between the excursive and discursive groups. They might stem from strongly held views about children's capacities. Whereas changing the mothers in the excursive group would involve sensitivity training, changing the mothers in the recursive group would involve undermining an existing ideology!

Although the previous section discussed what reducing variations in mother – child conversation would involve, it avoided the politically and morally contentious issue of whether reducing variations would be desirable. Perhaps the most significant factor in determining desirability is the extent to which children are disadvantaged by participating in conversations like the excursive and recursive groups. The degree of disadvantage depends partly on whether mother – child conversation affects skill at performing communicative functions other than providing information. Clearly, it has every opportunity to do so. In the first place, the performance of several other communicative functions can involve mentioning names, non-names and feature combinations. As the mothers' speech in (7.8) and (7.9) shows, names, non-names and feature combinations can be mentioned in the course of directing behaviour and requesting information:

(7.8)   [Mother gives model fireman to Philip (21.8)]
     Mother: Hold him there.
     Philip: No.
               That.
     [Philip drops model fireman]
     Mother: You brat.
               Put the hat on.
               You do it.
               Put the new hat on.

(7.9) [Eileen (23:18) looks at picture on blocks]
    Eileen: What's that?
    Mother: It's a train, isn't it?
            Where does a train go?
    Eileen: Swish-swish.
    Mother: What's that one?
    Eileen: A gee-gee.
            Dolly.
    Mother: Uhm.
            Look, there's a little teddy.
            What's the teddy sitting on?
    Eileen: Car.

In the second place, the performance of these other functions by young children leaves a lot to be desired. The observational studies of Greenfield and Smith (1976) and Halliday (1975) suggest that children in the present age range do not use solitary nouns only to provide information. They often use solitary nouns accompanied by whimpers and other unmistakable cues, as in (7.10), to direct behaviour:

(7.10) [Graham (20:19) discovers my toys prematurely]
    Graham: Box.
              Box.
              Box. Box.
              Box. Box. Box.
              Eh box.
    Mother: You're like a chorus, aren't you?
              Go and play with the other box.
    [Graham sobs]
    Graham: Box.
              Box.

Correspondingly, the work of Brown (1968), Klima and Bellugi (1966) and Labov and Labov (1978) suggests that early requests for information are predominantly concerned with object names. The child's remarks in (7.11) certainly concur with this:

(7.11) [Melanie (23:15) picks model hippo up]
    Melanie: What's that?
              What's that?
    Mother: Oh that's a hippo.
    Melanie: What's that?
    Mother: That's a hippo.

Thus, directing behaviour and requesting information can involve names, non-names and feature combinations. Moreover, there are obvious limitations on the names, non-names and feature combinations young children use to direct behaviour and request information. In the light of this, it seems appropriate to ask whether the speed with which children incorporate new names, non-names and feature combinations into their attempts to provide information is reflected in the speed with which they incorporate these phenomena into their attempts to direct behaviour and request information. The aim of the present section is to discuss this question.

(a) Theoretical considerations

To most linguists and many psycholinguists, its answer is self-evident. Skill at mentioning names, non-names and feature combinations while providing information is inextricably bound up with skill at mentioning names, non-names and feature combinations while performing other functions. This is because the names, non-names and feature combinations used to perform one communicative function are not thought to be stored separately from the names, non-names and feature combinations used to perform others. Rather, speakers have one store of nouns for naming objects and one store of linguistically encodable non-names and their potential combinations. These can be used in performing any communicative function. Of course, there has been much disagreement about the nature of these stores. For instance, Katz and Fodor (1963) believed that nouns were stored in a 'dictionary' that specified their grammatical role via 'syntactic markers' and their semantic content via 'semantic markers' and 'distinguishers'. Semantic markers were believed to specify universally accepted features whereas distinguishers were seen as more culturally specific. In the absence of independent evidence about which features are universally accepted, Bollinger (1965) has challenged the need for two semantic notions. Hence, other writers specify nouns purely in terms of syntactic and semantic features. A similar level of controversy exists over the specification of non-names and feature combinations. Virtually all theorists accept that linguistically encodable features of objects and their legitimate combination are specified in a single 'semantic component'. They disagree about details of specification. Linguists such as Chafe (1970) and Fillmore (1970) feel that the basic features are the potential for acting as agents, instruments, recipients and results of actions and locations and recipients of objects. Students of child language such as Bloom (1970), Brown (1973), Edwards (1973), Schlesinger (1971) and Slobin (1970) believe notions relating to owners and properties are equally fundamental.

It would be possible to write at length about the merits and demerits of these positions. In fact, books have been written on the subject. Despite its theoretical interest however, further discussion would digress too far. For present purposes, it is sufficient to note the level at which disagreement is pitched. Having done this, it is more important to focus on the point of general agreement, namely that stores of nouns for naming objects and features for conceptualizing objects transcend their communicative function. It is important, because this view (though indubitably true for adults) may be an oversimplification for young children. As pointed out in Chapter 5, there is no reason to suppose that children are interested in language *per se*. They are primarily interested in communication, viewing language as a tool in the service of communication. Chapter 5 argued the point on theoretical grounds, emphasizing that pre-school children are intellectually incapable of a non-pragmatic approach to knowledge. The point can also be supported empirically. The work of such writers as Bates *et al.* (1975) and Halliday (1975) has shown that children provide information and direct behaviour months before they learn conventional expressions. Bates *et al.* (1975) emphasized the use of gestures, describing how a 12-month-old girl used pointing, staring and even the motions of physical objects to direct her mother's behaviour. Halliday (1975) was more concerned with sounds, reporting how a 10-month-old boy used 'Nah' to demand objects and 'Ah' to report enjoyment. If children see linguistic expressions as tools for commuication, they must learn new aspects, including new names, non-names and feature combinations, with the intention of improving skill at performing particular communicative functions. Hence, every acquisition must initially be tied to particular functions, implying discrepancies at any given time between the names, non-names and feature combinations used to provide information, and the names, non-names and feature combinations used to perform other functions. Only gradually will acquisitions be generalized to other functions.

Although this suggestion may seem outrageous from a linguistic point of view, it is no more than an extension of Piaget's theory of general intellectual development. From historical syntheses of Piaget's writings, such as Gruber and Vonèche (1977), it is clear that Piaget has always seen intelligence as an integrated set of structures or 'schemes' that can be used to cope with particular problems. As a result, intellectual development is necessarily a twofold process, involving both the refinement of specific schemes and the integration of several schemes. In one of his clearest accounts of the first process, Piaget (1953) points out that the utilization of schemes has two aspects, which he calls 'assimilation' and 'accommodation'. Assimilation involves realizing which schemes are required for particular problems. For instance, realizing that extracting liquid from a cup involves grasping rather than dropping, and that checking bank statements involves adding rather than multiplying. Accommodation involves adapting the schemes to the demands of particular problems. For instance, adapting grasps to particular cups and additions to particular figures. At times, the demands of particular problems will be too great for pre-existing schemes. In Piaget's terms, a state of disequilibrium prevails between assimilation and accommodation. Equilibrium can be re-established by changing the scheme to cope with the problem, leading to the first developmental process. However, development of one scheme does not immediately produce development of other schemes. As Piaget himself has shown, children who accept that quantity is invariant when plasticine is rolled from a ball into a sausage do not necessarily accept that quantity is invariant when liquid is poured from a thin beaker into a fat beaker. Thus, a second developmental process is invoked to explain the gradual reduction of conflict, and increase in coordination, between schemes. The two developmental processes are encapsulated in Piaget's revised concept of 'equilibration', which has recently been presented by Furth (1980).

(b) Empirical evidence

The parallels between Piaget's theory and the present ideas about language development are probably clear. The present concern is with schemes underlying the various communicative functions. These schemes will be modified when they prove inadequate for particular communicative functions. Modification in the schemes underlying one communicative function will set up tensions in the schemes underlying others. These tensions will be gradually resolved, leading eventually, but not immediately, to the integrated system presupposed by linguists. Given these parallels, the evidence that Piaget invoked to support his second developmental process suggests the kind of evidence that might be invoked to support the present ideas. Piaget invoked the initially restricted use of advanced schemes. Corresponding evidence in the present context would be functionally restricted use of newly acquired linguistic skills. Perhaps surprisingly, such evidence seems to be available.

The study reported by Halliday (1975) has already been mentioned in several places. This study was based on functional and structural analyses of one child's communicative expressions. Reviewing the data used in these analyses highlights two points. Firstly, some expressions were restricted to single communicative functions throughout the first six months of the study (which started when the child was 9 months old). Secondly, some expressions were initially used for one communicative function before being generalized to others. For instances 'Pitta' was initially used to draw attention to the child's potty. A month later, it was also used to demand the potty. In his doctoral dissertation, Barrett (1979) describes how 'On here' and 'There' were first used directively and then generalized to other communicative functions. Finally, Bloom (1970) described the use of 'No' in the latter part of the second year. Her observations, which have been generally endorsed by Greenfield and Smith (1976), suggest that 'No' is initially an expression of rejection. Rejection is, of course, a subcategory of direction. Gradually 'No' is also used to deny truth and existence. Denial provides a certain kind of information.

Mentioning the work of Greenfield and Smith (1976) suggests one possible objection to the present line of reasoning. Greenfield and Smith were struck by certain assymetries in children's single-word utterances. For instance, children who can only manage single-word utterances must choose whether to label directions or objects when directing behaviour towards objects. Greenfield and Smith found their 18-month-old subjects habitually labelling directions when rejecting (via 'No') and objects when demanding (via nouns). They suggested the children's behaviour was governed by a principle of 'informativeness'. Children labelled the most uncertain aspect of the situation: non-occurring actions or unpossessed objects. At first sight, it might seem as if the principle of informativeness could explain why expressions are used in functionally restricted contexts. On further reflection, the principle could not explain why identical expressions are eventually used in prohibited contexts.

Of course, the notion that linguistic phenomena are initially tied to particular communicative functions and gradually extended elsewhere has profound implications for both the description and measurement of language development. More specifically, it implies some uncertainty about answering the question that initiated the present discussion. This was whether the speed with which new names, non-names and feature combinations are incorporated into attempts to provide information is reflected in the speed with which these phenomena are incorporated into attempts to perform other communicative functions. Given the present perspective, the answer must depend on the speed with which children resolve contradictions between the names, non-names and feature combinations they can provide, and the names, non-names and feature combinations they can use elsewhere. Who knows whether the rapid development of skill at providing information leads to rapid, average or slow resolution of contradictions with other skills? Children who rapidly develop skill at providing information might be so interested in this aspect of communication that they resolve contradictions more slowly than other children! Far fetched though this might seem, it is not beyond the realms of possibility. Nelson (1973a) divided her sample of 18 children into a 'referential' and an 'expressive' group. Her distinction has since been replicated by Bloom *et al.* (1975) and Barrett (1979). Although the groups were established on grammatical criteria, it seems as if the referential group were like the children in the discursive group. They were relatively quick to develop their skill at providing information. Interestingly, the characteristics of the expressive group suggest that children who are relatively slow to develop skill at providing information are relatively quick to develop skill at directing behaviour.

The intention in making these points is not to draw firm conclusions. It is rather to stress the inadvisability of drawing any conclusions about the inter-relatedness of communicative development. Without further research, it is quite impossible to say whether the superiority of the children in the discursive group was specific to skill at providing information or more general. Hence, it is equally impossible to say whether any advantages they derived from their conversational experiences were consolidated or nullified in other areas of language development. In which case, any suggestion that the mothers in the excursive and recursive groups emulate the mothers in the discursive group would be doubly misleading. In the first place, the impact of mother – child conversation on skill at providing information has still to be firmly established. In the second, the relationship between skill at providing information and performing other communicative functions remains uncertain. However, the research reported in this book was never intended to make practical suggestions. Instead, it was meant to clarify the nature of mother – child conversation and put forward some proposals about its developmental significance. Hopefully, it has partially succeeded in both aims. Hopefully too, it has suggested new areas of research and new approaches to research, not only within the field of mother – child conversation as a result of this chapter but also beyond. In its emphasis on both the heterogeneity and motivational significance of one aspect of the linguistic environment, it must surely have implications for the study of others.

References

Anglin, J. M. (1977). *Word, object and conceptual development*. Norton, New York.

Barrett, M. D. (1978). Lexical development and overextension in child language. *Journal of Child Language* **5**, 205–219.

Barrett, M. D. (1979). *Semantic development during the single-word stage of language acquisition*. Unpublished doctoral dissertation, University of Sussex.

Bates, E., Camaioni, L. and Volterra, V. (1975). The acquisition of performatives prior to speech. *Merrill-Palmer Quarterly* **21**, 205–226.

Bernstein, B. (1971). *Class, codes and control I: theoretical studies towards a sociology of language*. Routledge & Kegan Paul, London.

Bever, T. G. (1970). The cognitive basis for linguistic structures. *In* J. R. Hayes (Ed), *Cognition and the development of language*. Wiley, New York.

Bloom, L. (1970). *Language development: form and function in emerging grammars*. M.I.T. Press, Cambridge, Massachusetts.

Bloom, L. (1973). *One word at a time: the use of single-word utterances before syntax*. Mouton, The Hague.

Bloom, L., Hood, L. and Lightbown, P. (1974). Imitation in language development: if, when and why. *Cognitive Psychology* **6**, 380–420.

Bloom, L., Lightbown, P. and Hood, L. (1975). Structure and variation in child language. *Monographs of the Society for Research in Child Development* **40**, No. 8.

Bollinger, D. (1965). The atomization of meaning. *Language* **41**, 555–573.

Bowerman, M. (1973). *Early syntactic development: a cross-linguistic study with special reference to Finnish*. Cambridge University Press, Cambridge.

Braine, M.D.S. (1963). The ontogeny of English phrase structure: the first phase. *Language* **39**, 1–14.

Broen, P. A. (1972). The verbal environment of the language-learning child. *American Speech and Hearing Association Monograph*, No. 7.

Brown, R. (1957). *Words and things*. Free Press, Glencoe, Ill.

Brown, R. (1968). The development of wh-questions in child speech. *Journal of Verbal Learning and Verbal Behaviour* **7**, 279–290.

Brown, R. (1973). *A first language: the early stages*. George Allen & Unwin, London.

Brown, R. and Bellugi, U. (1964). Three processes in the child's acquisition of syntax. *Harvard Educational Review* **34**, 133–151.

Brown, R. and Ford, M. (1961). Address in American English. *Journal of Abnormal and Social Psychology* **62**, 375–385.

Brown, R. and Fraser, C. (1963). The acquisition of syntax. *In* C. N. Cofer and B. S. Musgrave, *Verbal behaviour and learning: problems and processes*. McGraw Hill, New York.

Brown, R., Cazden, C. and Bellugi-Klima, U. (1969). The child's grammar from I to III. *In* J. P. Hill (Ed), *Minnesota Symposia on Child Psychology*. University of Minnesota Press, Minneapolis.

Bruner, J. S. (1975a). The ontogenesis of speech acts. *Journal of Child Language* **2**, 1–19.

Bruner, J. S. (1975b). From communication to language — a psychological perspective. *Cognition* **3**, 255–287.

Bruner, J. S. (1977). Early social interaction and language acquisition. *In* H. R. Schaffer (Ed), *Studies in mother-infant interaction*. Academic Press, London.

Buffery, A. W. H. and Gray, J. A. (1972). Sex differences in the development of spatial and linguistic skills. *In* C. Ounstead and D. C. Taylor (Eds), *Gender differences: their ontogeny and significance*. Williams & Wilkins, Baltimore.

Cazden, C. (1970). The neglected situation in child language research and education. *In* F. Williams, (Ed), *Language and poverty: perspectives on a theme.* Markham, Chicago.

Chafe, W. L. (1970). *Meaning and the structure of language.* Chicago University Press, Chicago.

Clark, E. V. (1973). What's in a word? On the child's acquisition of semantics in his first language. *In* T. E. Moore (Ed), *Cognitive development and the acquisition of language.* Academic Press, New York.

Clark, E. V. (1978). Strategies of communicating. *Child Development* 49, 953–959.

Coulthard, M. (1977). *An introduction to discourse analysis.* Longman, London.

Cross, T. G. (1977). Mothers's speech adjustments: the contribution of selected child listener variables. *In* C. E. Snow and C. A. Ferguson (eds), *Talking to children: language input and acquisition.* Cambridge University Press, Cambridge.

Cross, T. G. (1978). Mothers' speech and its association with rate of linguistic development in young children. *In* N. Waterson and C. Snow, (Eds), *The development of communication.* John Wiley & Sons, Chichester.

Dore, J. (1974). A pragmatic description of early language development. *Journal of Psycholinguistic Research* 3, 343–350.

Dore, J. (1975). Holophrases, speech acts and language universals. *Journal of Child Language* 2, 21–40.

Downes, W. (1977). The imperative and pragmatics. *Journal of Linguistics* 13, 77–97.

Edwards, D. (1973). Sensorimotor intelligence and semantic relations in early child grammar. *Cognition* 2, 395–434.

Ervin, S. M. (1964). Imitation and structural change in children's language. *In* E. H. Lenneberg (Ed), *New directions in the study of language.* M.I.T. Press, Cambridge, Massachusetts.

Ervin-Tripp. S. M. (1969). Sociolinguistics. *In* L. Berkowitz (Ed), *Advances in experimental social psychology* 4, 93–107.

Ervin-Tripp, S. M. (1970). Discourse agreement: how children answer questions. *In* J. R. Hayes (Ed), *Cognition and the development of language.* Wiley, New York.

Ervin-Tripp, S. M. (1976). Is Sybil there? The structure of some American English directives. *Language in Society* 5, 25–66.

Fillmore, C. J. (1970). The case for case. *In* E. Bach and R. T. Harms (Eds), *Universals in linguistic theory.* Holt, Rinehart & Winston, London.

Fraser, C., Bellugi, U. and Brown, R. (1963). Control of grammar in imitation, comprehension and production. *Journal of Verbal Learning and Verbal Behaviour* 2, 121–135.

Furth. H. G. (1980). Piagetian perspectives. *In* H. J. Sants (Ed), *Developmental psychology and society.* Macmillan, London.

Gewirtz, J. L. and Gewirtz, H. B. (1965). Stimulus conditions, infant behaviors and social learning in four Israeli child rearing environments: a preliminary report illustrating differences in environment and behavior between the 'only' and the 'youngest' child. *In* B. F. Foss (Ed), *Determinants of infant behaviour III.* Methuen, London.

Gewirtz, H. B. and Gewirtz, J. L. (1969). Caretaking settings, background events and behavior differences in four Israeli child rearing environments: some preliminary trends. *In* B. M. Foss (Ed), *Determinants of infant behaviour IV.* Methuen, London.

Gordon, D. and Lakoff, G. (1971). Conversational postulates. Paper presented at Regional Meeting of Chicago Linguistic Society.

Greenfield, P. M. and Smith, J. H. (1976). *The structure of communication in early language development.* Academic Press, New York.

Gruber, H. E. and Vonèche, J. J. (1977). *The essential Piaget: an interpretative reference and guide.* Routledge & Kegan Paul, London.

Halliday, M. A. K. (1975). *Learning how to mean—explorations in the development of language.* Edward Arnold, London.

Harré, R. and DeWaele, J. P. (1976). The ritual for incorporation of a stranger. *In* R. Harré (Ed), *Life sentences: aspects of the social role of language.* Wiley, London.

Heinicke, C. M. (1956). Some effects of separating two-year old children from their parents: a comparative study. *Human Relations* 9, 105–176.

Holzman, M. (1972). The use of interrogative forms in the verbal interactions of three mothers and their children. *Journal of Psycholinguistic Research* 1, 311–336.

Holzman, M. (1974). The verbal environment provided by mothers for their very young children. *Merrill-Palmer Quarterly* 20, 31–42.

Howe, C. J. (1975). The nature and origin of social class differences in the propositions expressed by young children. Unpublished doctoral dissertation, University of Cambridge.

Howe, C. J. (1976). The meanings of two-word utterances in the speech of young children. *Journal of Child Language* 3, 29–47.

Howe, C. J. (1977). Review of 'P. M. Greenfield and J. H. Smith, The structure of communication in early language development'. *Journal of Child Language* 4, 479–483.

Howe, C. J. (1978). Review of 'J. M. Anglin, Word, object and conceptual development'. *Journal of Child Language* 5, 536–539.

Howe, C. J. (1979) Sensorimotor development, semantic competence and mother–child conversation. *In* M. Brenner (Ed), *Proceedings of Summer School of European Association of Experimental Social Psychology*, Oxford.

Howe, C. J. (1980a). Mother – child conversation and semantic development. *In* H. Giles, W. Robinson and P. Smith (Eds), *Language: Social Psychological Perspectives.* Pergamon Press, Oxford.

Howe, C. J. (1980b). Learning language from mothers' replies. *First Language*, 1, 83–98.

Inhelder, B. and Piaget, J. (1958). *The early growth of logic in the child.* Routledge & Kegan Paul, London.

Jaffe, J. and Feldstein, S. (1970). *Rhythms of dialogue.* Academic Press, New York.

Kagan, J. (1971). *Change and continuity in infancy.* Wiley, New York.

Katz, J. J. and Fodor, J. A. (1963). The structure of a semantic theory. *Language* 39, 170–210.

Keenan, E. O. (1977). Making it last: repetition in children's discourse. *In* S. M. Ervin-Tripp and C. Mitchell-Kernan (Eds), *Child discourse.* Academic Press, New York.

Keenan, E. O. and Schieffelin, B. B. (1976). Topic as a discourse notion: a study of topic in the conversation of children and adults. *In* C. Li (Ed), *Subject and topic.* Academic Press, New York.

Kendon, A. (1967). Some functions of gaze direction in social interaction. *Acta Psychologia* 26, 22–63.

Klima, E. S. and Bellugi, U. (1966). Syntactic regularities in the speech of children. *In* J. Lyons and R. J. Wales (Eds), *Psycholinguistic Papers.* Edinburgh University Press, Edinburgh.

Kohl, J. A. and Davis, J. A. (1955). A comparison of indexes of socio-economic status. *American Sociological Review* 20, 317–325.

Labov, W. (1972). Rules for ritual insults. *In* D. Sudnow (Ed), *Studies in social interaction*. The Free Press, New York.

Labov, W. and Labov, T. (1978) Learning the syntax of questions. *In* R. N. Campbell and P. T. Smith (Eds), *Recent advances in the psychology of language: formal and experimental approaches*. Plenum, New York.

Lakoff, R. (1974). Why women are ladies. *Berkeley Studies in Syntax and Semantics* 1, No. XV.

Lawson, E. D. and Boek, W. E. (1960). Correlations of indexes of families' socio-economic status. *Social Forces* 39, 149–152.

Leach, G. M. (1972). A comparison of the social behaviour of some normal and problem children. *In* N. Blurton-Jones (Ed), *Ethological studies of child behaviour*. Cambridge University Press, Cambridge.

Lenneberg, E. H. (1964). A biological perspective of language. *In* E. H. Lenneberg (Ed) *New directions in the study of language*. M.I.T. Press, Cambridge, Massachusetts.

Lenneberg, E. H. (1967). *Biological foundations of language*. Wiley, New York.

Leonard, L. B. and Kaplan, L. (1976). A note on imitation and lexical acquisition. *Journal of Child Language* 3, 449–455.

Leopold, W. E. (1939). *Speech development of a bilingual child. Vol. 1, Vocabulary growth in the first two years*. Northwestern University, Evanston, Ill.

Lieven, E. V. M. (1972). *Language acquisition in the young child*. Paper submitted to Churchill College Fellowship Electors, Cambridge.

Lieven, E. V. M. (1978a). Conversations between mothers and young children: individual differences and their possible implications for the study of language learning. *In* N. Waterson and C. Snow (Eds), *The development of communication*. John Wiley & Sons, Chichester.

Lieven, E. V. M. (1978b). Turn-taking and pragmatics: two issues in early child language. *In* R. N. Campbell and P. T. Smith (Eds), *Recent advances in the psychology of language: language development and mother – child interaction*. Plenum, New York.

Lovell, K. and Dixon, E. M. (1965). The growth of the control of grammar in imitation, comprehension and production. *Journal of Child Psychology and Psychiatry* 5, 1–9.

Maccoby, E. E. and Jacklin, C. N. (1975). *The psychology of sex differences*. Oxford University Press, London.

McNeill, D. (1966a). The creation of language. *Discovery* 27, 34–38.

McNeill, D. (1966b). Developmental psycholinguistics. *In* F. Smith and G. A. Miller (Eds), *The genesis of language: a psycholinguistic approach*. M.I.T. Press, Cambridge, Massachusetts.

McNeill, D. (1970). *The acquisition of language: the study of developmental psycholinguistics*. Harper & Row, New York.

McTear, M. (1978). Repetition in child language: imitation or creation? *In* R. N. Campbell and P. T. Smith (Eds), *Recent advances in the psychology of language: language development and mother – child interaction*. Plenum, New York.

Menyuk, P. (1969). *Sentences children use*. M.I.T. Press, Cambridge, Massachusetts.

Messer, D. J. (1978). The integration of mothers' referential speech with joint play. *Child Development* 49, 781–787.

Moerk, E. L. (1972). Principles of dyadic interaction in language learning. *Merrill-Palmer Quarterly* 18, 229–257.

Moerk, E. L. (1974). Changes in verbal child – mother interaction with increasing language skills of the child. *Journal of Psycholinguistic Research* 3, 101–116.

Moerk, E. L. (1975). Verbal interaction between children and their mothers during the preschool years. *Developmental Psychology* **11**, 788–794.

Moerk, E. L. (1976). Processes of language teaching and training in the interaction of mother – child dyads. *Child Development* **47**, 1064–1078.

Nelson, K. (1973a). Structure and strategy in learning to talk. *Monographs of the Society for Research in Child Development* **38**, Nos 1–2.

Nelson, K. (1973b). Some evidence for the cognitive primacy of categorization and its functional basis. *Merrill-Palmer Quarterly* **19**, 21–39.

Nelson, K., Rescorla, L., Gruendel, J. and Benedict, H. (1978). Early lexicons: what do they mean? *Child Development* **49**, 960–968.

Nelson, K. E., Carskaddon, G. and Bonvillian, J. D. (1973). Syntax acquisition: impact of experimental variation in adult verbal interaction with the child. *Child Development* **44**, 497–504.

Ninio, A. and Bruner, J. S. (1978). The achievement and antecedents of labelling. *Journal of Child Language* **5**, 1–15.

Phillips, J. (1973). Syntax and vocabulary of mothers' speech to young children: age and sex comparisons. *Child Development* **44**, 182–185.

Piaget, J. (1926). *The language and thought of the child.* Routledge & Kegan Paul, London.

Piaget, J. (1953). *The origins of intelligence in the child.* Routledge & Kegan Paul, London.

Piaget, J. (1955). *The child's construction of reality.* Routledge & Kegan Paul, London.

Piaget, J. (1962). *Play, dreams and imitation in childhood.* Norton, New York.

Piaget, J. and Inhelder, B. (1956). *The child's conception of space.* Routledge & Kegan Paul, London.

Remick, H. (1976). Maternal speech to children during language acquisition. *In* W. Van Raffler-Engel and Y. Lebrun (Eds), *Baby talk and infant speech.* Swetz & Zeitlinger, Amsterdam.

Richards, M. P. M. and Bernal, J. (1972). An observational study of mother-infant interaction. *In* N. Blurton-Jones (Ed), *Ethological studies of child behaviour.* Cambridge University Press, Cambridge.

Ringler, N. (1978). A longitudinal study of mothers' language. *In* N. Waterson and C. Snow (Eds), *The development of communication.* John Wiley & Sons, Chichester.

Rodd, L. J. and Braine, M. D. S. (1971). Children's imitation of syntactic constructions as a measure of linguistic competence, *Journal of Verbal Learning and Verbal Behaviour* **10**, 430–443.

Rodgon, M. M. (1976). *Single-word usage, cognitive development and the beginnings of combinatorial speech: a study of English-speaking children.* Cambridge University Press, Cambridge.

Ryan, J. F. (1973). Interpretation and imitation in early language development. *In* R. Hinde and J. S. Hinde (Eds), *Constraints on learning: limitations and predispositions.* Academic Press, London.

Sachs, J., Brown, R. and Salerno, R. (1976). Adult speech to children. *In* W. Van Raffler-Engel and Y. Lebrun (Eds), *Baby talk and infant speech.* Swetz & Zeitlinger, Amsterdam.

Sacks, H. (1972). An initial investigation of the usability of conversational data for doing sociology. *In* D. Sudnow (Ed), *Studies in social interaction.* The Free Press, New York.

Sacks, H. Schegloff, E. A. and Jefferson, G. (1974). A simplest systematics for the organization of turn-taking for conversation. *Language* **50**, 696–735.

Savic, S. (1975). Aspects of adult – child communication: the problem of question acquisition. *Journal of Child Language* **2**, 251–260.

Schaffer, H. R. and Crook, C. K. (1979). The role of the mother in early social development. *In* H. McGurk (Ed), *Childhood social development*. Methuen, London.

Schegloff, E. A. and Sacks, H. (1973). Opening up closings. *Semiotica* **8**, 289–327.

Schlesinger, I. M. (1971). Production of utterances and language acquisition. *In* D. I. Slobin (Ed). *The ontogenesis of grammar*. Academic Press, New York.

Searle, J. R. (1969). *Speech acts: an essay in the philosophy of language*. Cambridge University Press, London.

Seitz, S. and Stewart, C. (1975). Imitation and expansion: some developmental aspects of mother-child conversation. *Developmental Psychology* **11**, 763–768.

Shatz, M. (1978). Children's comprehension of their mothers' question-directives. *Journal of Child Language* **5**, 39–46.

Siegel, S. (1956). *Non-parametric statistics for the behavioural sciences*. McGraw-Hill, New York.

Sinclair, H. (1969). Developmental psycholinguistics. *In* D. Elkind and J. H. Flavell (Eds) *Studies in cognitive development: essays in honor of Jean Piaget*. Oxford University Press, New York.

Sinclair, H. (1971). Sensorimotor action patterns as a condition for the acquisition of syntax. *In* R. Huxley and E. Ingram (Eds), *Language acquisition: models and methods*. Academic Press, London.

Sinclair, H. (1973). Some remarks on the Genevan point of view on learning with special reference to language learning. *In* R. Hinde and J. S. Hinde (Eds), *Constraints on learning: limitations and predispositions*. Academic Press, London.

Slobin, D. I. (1968). Imitation and grammatical development in children. *In* N. S. Endler, L. R. Boulter and H. Osser (Eds), *Contemporary issues in developmental psychology*. Holt, Rinehart & Winston, New York.

Slobin, D. I. (1970). Universals of grammatical development. *In* G. B. Flores D'Arcais and W. J. M. Levelt (Eds), *Advances in psycholinguistics*. North-Holland, Amsterdam.

Smilansky, S. (1968). *The effects of sociodramatic play on disadvantaged preschool children*. John Wiley & Sons, New York.

Snow, C. E. (1972). Mothers' speech to children learning language. *Child Development* **43**, 549–565.

Snow, C. E. (1977a). The development of conversation between mothers and babies. *Journal of Child Language* **4**, 1–22.

Snow, C. E. (1977b). Mothers' speech research: from input to interaction. *In* C. E. Snow and C. A. Ferguson (Eds), *Talking to children: language input and acquisition*. Cambridge University Press, Cambridge.

Snow, C. E., Arlmann-Rupp, A., Hassing, Y., Jobse, J., Joosten, J. and Vorster, J. (1976). Mothers' speech in three social classes. *Journal of Psycholinguistic Research* **5**, 1–20.

Sugarman-Bell, S. (1978). Some organizational aspects of pre-verbal communication. *In* I. Marková (Ed). *The social context of language*. John Wiley & Sons, Chichester.

Trevarthen, C. (1975). Early attempts at speech. *In* R. Lewin (Ed), *Child alive: new insights into the development of young children*. Temple Smith, London.

Trevarthen, C. (1977). Descriptive analysis of infant communicative behaviour. *In* H. R. Schaffer (Ed), *Studies in mother-infant interaction.* Academic Press, London.

Walters, J., Connor, R. and Zunich, M. (1964). Interaction of mothers and children from lower class families. *Child Development* **35**, 433–440.

Wells, G. (1974). Learning to code experience through language. *Journal of Child Language* **1**, 243–269.

Wells, G. (1979). *Adjustments in adult–child conversation.* Paper presented at Social Psychology and Language Conference, Bristol.

Appendix: Object Names and Non-names Used by Some Children

Object names

Wayne

1st Recording
Baby (10)
A baby (9)
Bag (4)
A bag (1)
Ball (2)
A ball (8)
Is ball (1)
A bang (1)
Bird (1)
A bird (2)
Bow-wow (12)
A bow-wow (4)
Car (2)
A car (2)
Dada (14)
A dada (11)
Dog (1)
A dog (4)
Doodle-doo (16)
A doodle-doo (12)
Door (2)
A door (8)
A gogga (2)
Man (9)
A man (4)
Nana (9)
A nana (2)
Nose (1)
Shoe (2)
A wee-wee (2)

2nd Recording
Baby (47)
A baby (4)
Ball (4)
A ball (2)
Is ball (1)
Is a ball (1)
There ball (1)
A bath (1)
Book (9)
There book (2)
Bow-wow (17)
A bow-wow (2)
Here bow-wow (1)
Car (10)
Coat (3)
Dolly (2)
Doodle-doo (5)
A doodle-doo (1)
Door (8)
An door (2)
There door (1)
Ear (1)
Gee-gee (1)
Girl (1)
A gogga (1)
Here gogga (1)
Lady (1)
Lalla (21)
Lorry (6)
A lorry (3)

Man (15)
Man there (6)
A man (5)
The man (2)
Nana (6)
A nana (1)
Here nana in there (1)
There nana (1)
Nose (1)
Plate (1)
Shoe (4)
Shoes (3)
A shoe (2)
A shoes (1)
Here shoes (1)
Spoon (6)
Sugar (1)
Tea (2)
Teddy (1)
Toot-toot (1)
Tune (4)
A tune (1)
Wool (1)

Ian

1st Recording
Animals (2)
Baby (1)

143

Bear that (1)
Boat (1)
Boxes (3)
Camel (2)
Car (5)
Cars (6)
No car (1)
That car (1)
Carpark (1)
Clock on (1)
Colours (1)
That colour (1)
Dadda (2)
Doggie (1)
Dougall (3)
Elephant (5)
Eye (1)
Face (1)
Garage (3)
House (7)
There house (1)
Mouth (3)
Nana (1)
Nana there (1)
Nose (1)
Penguin (1)
There penguin (1)
Puzzle (1)
Rabbit (1)
Sheep (1)
Top (1)
Trousers (1)
Wee-wee (3)
Windows here (1)
Here windows (3)
There windows (3)

2nd Recording
Bomb (1)
Box (1)
Bread (1)
Breakfast (4)
Brush (2)
Bumpers on there (1)
Car (3)
Car on there (1)
That car (1)
It's chair (1)
Clock (1)

Cover (1)
Cup (3)
Dad (1)
Dinner (1)
Dolly there (2)
Dolly in there (2)
Door (3)
Doors (1)
Door there (2)
That's door (1)
Engine (2)
Fluff (1)
Garage (1)
That garage (1)
Gates (2)
Gates on it (2)
Grandma (1)
Hat (1)
That's hat (1)
House (1)
Man (1)
Milkcar (1)
Milkman (2)
Paint (1)
Plate (1)
Rabbit (1)
Spoon (2)
Sugar (1)
Teeth (1)
Tiger (1)
Trousers (1)
Water (1)
That windows (1)

Kevin

1st Recording
Baby (2)
Banana (1)
Bed (6)
A bed (1)
The bed (1)
Bottle (1)
Boy (2)
Bubble (2)
Cake (2)
Car (9)
A car (1)
Castle (1)

Clock (3)
Coffee (8)
Daddy (2)
Dolly (2)
Door (6)
Dougall (30)
Duck (4)
Dumplings (1)
Eyes (1)
Face (2)
Flower (1)
Fork (1)
Girl (1)
Grandma (1)
House (1)
Lid (6)
Man (4)
Milk (3)
Nose (1)
Paper (1)
Pencil (1)
Phone (1)
Rat (5)
Scissors (1)
See-saw (2)
Shells (1)
Shrub (2)
Slide (1)
Sock (1)
Star (1)
Sweet (3)
Tea (13)
Toe (7)
Tongue (1)
Tractor (9)
Train (1)
Tree (1)

2nd Recording
Baby (1)
Baby there (1)
A bag (1)
Basket (1)
A basket (2)
A bear (1)
Biscuits (1)
Boy (1)
Brush (1)
Car (3)
This car (1)

Castle (1)
Comb (2)
Cover (1)
Cream (1)
There dog (1)
Dolly (1)
Drawing (2)
That drawing (2)
Duck (2)
Eyes (1)
Grandma (1)
Hair (1)
Hand (1)
Horsie (2)
Jeffrey (2)
Johnny (2)
Lorry (1)
There's a man (1)
Nancy (1)
Panda (3)
Penguin (1)
People (1)
Pig (1)
Pushchair (1)
Pussy (1)
Shoes (1)
Shop (3)
Shops in there (1)
Shopping (7)
Shopping there (1)
It's shopping (1)
Sweeties (1)
Tea (1)
Teddy (2)
Telephone (2)
Tiger (2)
Tissues (1)
Towel (3)
Tractor (3)
Water (2)
Wheel (1)

Non-names (* denotes feature combinations)

Wayne

1st Recording
Go (2)

Go down (1)
Gone (2)
My doodle-doo (1)*

2nd Recording
Allgone (15)
Another (4)
On back (1)
On a back (1)
On the back (1)
Bath (1)
A bath (3)
The bath (2)
In bath (2)
In a bath (1)
In the bath (4)
Bitten (1)
In book (1)
In a book (1)
There bye-bye (1)
In car (1)
In the car (2)
Cut-cut (8)
In drawer (2)
In a drawer (1)
Fall down (2)
Find shoe (1)*
Gone (18)
Gone the back (1)*
Here gone (2)
No gone (3)
There gone (1)
In the lorry (1)
More (1)
No more (1)
My baby (1)*
Nana gone (1)*
Nice (1)
Some (1)

Ian

1st Recording
Baa sheep (2)*
Black (1)
Car garage (1)*
Dog on car (1)*
Fall (12)
Fall again (1)
Fall down (10)

That fall (1)
Finished (2)
Found it (1)
Funny (4)
Funny thingy's hat (1)*
Go on house (1)*
That goes (1)
There go on (1)
House fall (1)*
Looking (1)
Nice (1)
Posting box (1)*
Red (6)
Red car (5)*
That red (2)
Stuck (1)
Two (1)
Wrong (1)
Wrong place (2)*
Yellow (9)
That yellow (1)

2nd Recording
Allgone (1)
All in there (1)
Baby's hat (1)*
That backwards (1)
In bed (1)
Big house (1)*
Comb my hair (1)*
Crash (21)
Crash down (1)
Crash in garage (1)*
Crash off there (1)
Crash on top that man (1)*
Crash there (1)
Doing (1)
He doing teeth (1)*
That's doll's (1)
Fall down (1)
Fall down the road (1)*
Falled (2)
All falling down (1)
That falled (1)
Finish (1)
Finish now (2)
Going (14)
Going to a grandma (1)*
Going out (1)
Going school (1)*
Going somewhere (2)*

Going there (1)
Me going that backwards (1)*
That going (1)
Gone (1)
Knock people down (1)*
Little house (1)*
Lorry falled (1)*
More on that (2)
Open (1)
Play animal (1)*
I pulling on it (1)
Ride her (1)
That rocks (1)
Round (1)
All stand up (1)
Three (1)
Turned over (1)
Walking (1)
Wrong page (1)*
Wrong place (1)*

Kevin

1st Recording
On bed (1)
On the bed (1)
Blue hat (2)*
Broken (3)
It broke (1)
Katharine (1)
Kevin (6)
Knock (6)
Moo cow (1)*
Mummy (1)
Orange juice (1)*
Sleep (9)
Stuck (1)
Tea Kevin (2)*
Tea Nana (1)*
Teddy (4)

2nd Recording
Another (3)
Another book (1)*
Another cake (1)*
Baby socks (1)*
Beautiful (1)
He's big too (1)
Big load (1)*

Broken (3)
Buy some bananas (1)*
Buy sweeties (1)*
Car key (4)*
Clean (4)
Cold (3)
Cold water (1)*
Come (2)
Come now (2)
Cover down bed (1)*
Crash (1)
Dirty (1)
Door open (13)*
Door shut (10)*
Driving it (1)
Drop it (1)
Eating something (1)*
Elly stuck (1)*
Fall (1)
Fall down (2)
Filthy hair (1)*
Find (2)
Find another (2)*
Find there (1)
This find (1)
Fluffy (1)
Game (4)
Go there (1)
Grandma did (1)*
Ice cream (1)*
Jeffrey come (3)
Johnny come (3)*
Katharine did it (2)*
Kiss (1)
That kiss (1)
Knock down (2)
Later (1)
Little piggie (1)*
More (4)
More shop (1)*
Mummy cake (1)*
Names Kevin (1)*
Nancy gone (1)*
Panda cry (1)*
Party (2)
Poor duck (1)*
Poor man (1)*
Pussy cat (1)*
Raining (1)
Rosy (2)
Saw it (5)

Shopping later (2)
Sunny day (2)*
Sweet shop (1)*
Swimming (1)
Tip (2)
Tipper lorry (2)*
It's tipping lorry (1)*
Too windy (3)

Index